ENCYCLOPAEDIA OF EMINENT THINKERS

VOLUME - XXX: **SIR PHEROZESHAH MEHTA**

Volumes by the same author

The Political Thought of ***Dadabhai Naoroji***
The Political Thought of ***Tej Bahadur Sapru***
The Political Thought of ***C. Rajagopalachari***
The Political Thought of ***Subhas Chandra Bose***
The Political Thought of ***Bhagat Singh***
The Political Thought of ***Annie Besant***
The Political Thought of ***C.R. Das***
The Political Thought of ***Lala Lajpat Rai***
The Political Thought of ***Sir Pherozeshah Mehta***
The Political Thought of ***Mahadev Govind Ranade***

About the Author

Dr. (Miss) Ashu Pasricha is a faculty in Gandhian studies at Panjab University, Chandigarh. She has many books to her credit including *Gandhian Approach to Integrated Rural Development; Public Administration:* Discipline *and Dimensions; Peace Studies: Discipline and Dimensions;* WTO, *Self-reliance and Globalisation;* and *Gandhi's Concept of State and Power.* Also, she has published a number of research papers in various Indian and foreign journals of repute.

ENCYCLOPAEDIA OF EMINENT THINKERS

VOLUME- XXX

THE POLITICAL THOUGHT OF SIR PHEROZESHAH MEHTA

Dr. Ashu Pasricha
Department of Gandhian Studies
Panjab University
Chandigarh

CONCEPT PUBLISHING COMPANY, NEW DELHI-110 059

ISBN 13-978-81-7022-684-0 (Series) ISBN 10-81-7022-684-8 (Series)
ISBN 13-978-81-8069-638-1 (Vol. XXX) ISBN 10-81-8069-638-3 (Vol. XXX)

First Published 2010

Published and Printed by

Concept Since 1974

Concept Publishing Company

Regd. Office:

A/15-16, Commercial Block, Mohan Garden

New Delhi-110059 (India)

Phones : 25351460, 25351794, *Fax* : 091-11-25357109

Email : publishing@conceptpub.com,

Website: www.conceptpub.com

Editorial Office:

H-13, Bali Nagar, New Delhi-110 015, India.

Cataloging in Publication Data-- *Courtesy:* D.K. Agencies (P) Ltd. docinfo@dkagencies.com

Encyclopaedia of eminent thinkers.
v. 26-30 cm. -- (Gandhian studies and peace research series ; 11)
Vols. 11- lack series statement.
In Indian context.
Includes bibliographical references. Includes indexes.
Contents: v. 26. The political thought of C.R. Das / Ashu Pasricha -- v. 27 The political thought of Gopal Krishna Gokhale / Jai Narain Sharma -- v. 28. The political thought of Lala Lajpat Rai / Ashu Pasricha -- v. 29. The political thought of Maulana Abul Kalam Azad / Jai Narain Sharma - v. 30. The political thought of Sir Pherozeshah Mehta / Ashu Pasricha.
ISBN 13: 9788170226840 (set) ISBN 10: 8170226848 (set)

1. Statesmen--India. 2. Political science--India. 3. India--Politics and government. I. Sharma, Jai Narain, 1951- II. Pasricha, Ashu, 1967- III. Series: Gandhian studies and peace research series ; 11.

DDC 954.035 22

DEDICATED
TO
MY REVERED TEACHER
&
COLLEAGUE
PROFESSOR JAI NARAIN SHARMA
AND HIS WIFE
DR. RASHMI SHARMA

PREFACE

Pherozeshah was far and away the greatest political leader India has known. His supreme virtue was fearlessness. Once he made up his mind about some public question and defined his policy, he stuck to it with dauntless determination and no power on earth could dislodge him from his position. He never knew hesitation, equivocation or prevarication. His intellectual eminence, legal and constitutional acumen, and political shrewdness, shone all the ore brightly because of their foundation on resolutc intrepidity.

In assessing Pherozeshah's public career, it is essential to remember that many of his principles were formed by his early training and environment. He had the good fortune to receive his education at the hands of a scholar of great attainments and singular breadth of view. When he went to England, it was with a mind fully equipped to receive the ideas and impressions which the West has to impart. While studying for the Bar, he came under the influence of Dadabhai Naoroji, who inspired him with his own burning love of the country and enthusiasm for the cause of progress and liberty. The young disciple was deeply interested in the world around him, and the social and political forces that were at work.

Pherozeshah's temperament, equally with his early training was a great asset. He was a robust optimist and he faced the problems of the day with serene courage and confidence. The hatred of enemies, the indifference of friends and the hostility of those in power and authority failed to shake his faith in the ultimate triumph of the cause he had espoused, and in the principles and methods by which he pursued it.

He was a firm believer, like many others of his generation, in the benefit of the British connection. No man more mercilessly exposed the defects, shortcomings and injustice which have often characterised the British administration of India, no man more courageously fought for the enlargement of the rights and liberties of the people and yet there was none who upheld the British connection more stoutly then he, recognizing as he did the weakness of his country's position, and the essential justice and humanity, despite many lapses of England's rule in India. He had deep-seated respect for constituted authority, which his early training had implanted in him. This was most strikingly exemplified in his civic career. While there was no critique of the administration more fear less than he, the executive officers had no warmer supporters of their prestige and authority.

In an attempt to draw up the pen-picture of this illustrious leader, I must admit that in some places there ought to be some inferences, just to bring the facts of his life in the formation of a book. Collection of materials are in conformity with details published in different newspapers at different times.

Personal acknowledgements are no easy matters where so many have been kind. My special thanks are due to Professor R.N. Pal, Professor N. Radhakrishnan, Dr. K.S. Bharathi, Dr. A.D. Mishra, Professor Jai Narain Sharma, Dr. Meena Dutta, Dr. Seema Pasricha, Dr. Rashmi Sharma, Mr. Ajay Pasricha (Advocate) and Master Hemant Malhotra. Beyond that I can make only an all embracing salute to the galaxy of scholars whose works I have consulted.

I am also grateful to Shri Ashok Kumar Mittal, my publisher, for his consistent zeal in the printing and publication of this volume.

Chandigarh **ASHU PASRICHA**

CONTENTS

Encyclopaedia of Eminent Thinkers Series

Vol. I. The Political Thought of Mahatma Gandhi/ *K.S. Bharti*
Vol. II. The Political Thought of Nehru/ *K.S. Bharti*
Vol. III. The Political Thought of Rabindra Nath Tagore/ *K.S. Bharti*
Vol. IV. The Political Thought of Radhakrishnan/ *K.S. Bharti*
Vol. V. The Political Thought of Vinoba/ *K.S. Bharti*
Vol. VI. The Political Thought of Aurobindo/ *K.S. Bharti*
Vol. VII. The Political Thought of Jayaprakash Narayan/ *K.S. Bharti*
Vol. VIII. The Political Thought of Vivekananda/ *K.S. Bharti*
Vol. IX. The Political Thought of Ambedkar/ *K.S. Bharti*
Vol. X. The Political Thought of M.N. Roy/ *K.S. Bharti*
Vol. XI. The Political Thought of Dadabhai Naoroji/ *Ashu Pasricha*
Vol. XII. The Political Thought of Veer Savarkar/ *Jai Narain Sharma*
Vol. XIII. The Political Thought of M.A. Jinnah/ *Jai Narain Sharma*
Vol. XIV. The Political Thought of Tej Bahadur Sapru/ *Ashu Pasricha*
Vol. XV. The Political Thought of C. Rajagopalachari/ *AshuPasricha*
Vol. XVI. The Political Thought of Subhas Chandra Bose/ *Ashu Pasricha*
Vol. XVII. The Political Thought of Mohammad Iqbal/ *Jai Narain Sharma*
Vol. XVIII. The Political Thought of K.B. Hedgewar/ *Jai Narain Sharma*
Vol. XIX. The Political Thought of Bhagat Singh/ *Ashu Pasricha*
Vol. XX. The Political Thought of M.S. Golwalkar/ *Jai Narain Sharma*
Vol. XXI. The Political Thought of Sir Syed Ahmed Khan/ *Jai Narain Sharma*
Vol. XXII. The Political Thought of Mahadev Govind Ranade/ *Ashu Pasricha*
Vol. XXIII. The Political Thought of Pandit Deendayal Upadhyaya/ *Jai Narain Sharma*
Vol. XXIV. The Political Thought of Lokmanya Bal Gangadhar Tilak/ *Jai Narain Sharma*
Vol. XXV. The Political Thought of Annie Besant/ *Ashu Pasricha*
Vol. XXVI. The Political Thought of C.R. Das/ *Ashu Pasricha*
Vol. XXVII. The Political Thought of Gopal Krishna Gokhale/ *Jai Narain Sharma*
Vol. XXVIII. The Political Thought of Lala Lajpat Rai/ *Ashu Pasricha*
Vol. XXIX. The Political Thought of Maulana Abul Kalam Azad/ *Jai Narain Sharma*
Vol. XXX. The Political Thought of Sir Pherozeshah Mehta/ *Ashu Pasricha*

1

LIFE AND TIMES

Pherozeshah Mehta was born in Bombay on 4 August 1845. His father was a merchant who spent most of his life in Calcutta, and was at one time a partner in the well-known firm of P. & C.N. Cama & Co., which with many other business houses came to grief in the Share Mania of 1865. He was a man of means at the period of which we are speaking, and was able to bring up his children in comfort. Though not endowed with any education worth the name, he possessed some literary tastes, and was the author of a text-book on Geography and a Gujarati translation of some work on Chemistry. His brother Sorabji was a man of considerable ability, who held a responsible position in a banking concern, and was keenly interested in the social and educational questions of the day. The family lived in one of the localities in the Fort which were in those days inhabited by the wealthiest in the community, and most of which are now known only for their squalor and general indications of poverty. It is not necessary to delve deeper than this into the family history in order to trace influences of heredity or environment, which, as a present-day critic says, are often a snare to the biographer.

Pherozeshah's early education began in what was known as Ayrton's School. This was an institution established by Dhunjibhoy Cama, one of the partners of the elder Mehta, and honoured with the name of Ayrton, who was the family solicitor of the Camas, and who took a great interest in the education of boys. In those days, though there was not so much general intercourse between Englishmen and Indians as exists at present, there was much more of genuine friendship between individuals, and manifestations of friendly regard like the above were not unusual. In many cases the Parsis of those days adopted the surnames of their patrons or friends, and were known by the latter.

From Ayrton's school, Pherozeshah went in 1855 to that well known institution which was known as the "Branch School," the cradle of many distinguished men who have made history in Bombay. After six happy years spent in an irresponsible and happy go-lucky way, characteristic of all healthy-minded schoolboys, he passed the Matriculation, which had been instituted soon after the great charter of education of 1854 was brought into operation. Shortly after, he joined the Elphinstone College, then located at Gowalia, Tank Road, known as "Tankerville". It was an old and unpretentious building, immediately adjoining a large tank now filled in, but the grounds were spacious and full of trees. The surroundings were pleasant, and compared favourably with present-day conditions.

Of Pherozeshah's life at College, there is not much to be said. He was a keen and diligent student, particularly fond of history and English literature, and showed himself to be endowed with a mind of unusual capacity. His personality was striking. Though of little more than medium height, his strong and handsome features and broad shoulders lent considerable dignity and impressiveness to his general appearance. His conversation was brilliant, and drew towards him a large circle of friends. Among them were several, who in later years stood with him on the same platform on many an occasion, and fought under his banner. Young Pherozeshah also became a favourite with the great educationist who was at the helm of the institution, Sir Alexander Grant. One of the essays written by him so impressed the latter that it was ordered to be preserved in the archives of the College from which some devoted disciple may some day unearth it.

The culture imparted in those days was in many respects sounder, and took deeper root than modern conditions allow. The pupils were few and they came closely and directly under the influence of singularly able and conscientious teachers. Pherozeshah made the most of his opportunities. In the annual reports which were sent to his father over the signature of Sir Alexander, his conduct and progress were described as excellent. He was quick at grasping the salient points of the subject before him, but avoided the short-cuts to knowledge which such facility often encourages. He belonged to that somewhat rare type of men in whom great natural advantages are found allied with a capacity for taking pains.

While the cultivation of the mind was promoted in every way, the development of the body was not neglected. Though little inclined to any vigorous physical exertion, Pherozeshah was fond of cricket, and played a great deal of what was then a little known game. He is said to have played in characteristic fashion, never knowing when he was defeated. Sir Alexander was himself fond of the game, and encouraged its pursuit among his pupils. On one occasion, he even took a team with him to the Deccan, Pherozeshah forming one of the Eleven Later at College and other convivial gatherings, when old days were recalled with affection, Pherozeshah took a whimsical delight in claiming that he was one of the pioneers of the game, and in disputing with the late Jamsetjee Patel, his title as the Father of Indian Cricket, contending that long before the latter emerged on the scene, he and his contemporaries, proud of their bats and stumps which had been made by a native carpenter, used to indulge in the game in the *maidan* outside the ramparts of the old Fort, which had guarded the little town for generations, and which later had to be demolished with the rise of modern Bombay.[1]

Those years at college were well spent. They taught the young man to stand upright; they certainly fostered no "slave mentality". They were devoted to the cultivation of a mind which was very receptive, and to the pursuit of a healthy out-door life. The opportunities for the acquisition of culture which existed in those days, the attention that it was possible to bestow on each student, and the sympathetic understanding which existed between the professors and their pupils, all contributed to bring out the best that was in a man, and in such an atmosphere Pherozeshah's intellect ripened early. He had the rare advantage, besides, of coming under the influence of Sir Alexander Grant's inspiring personality, and the value of this early association he repeatedly acknowledged in after years.

In 1864, Pherozeshah passed his B.A. examination, and was awarded of Dakshiaa Fellowship by Sir Alexander, who was anxious to retain his connection with the college. About this time, he received a compliment which was as rare as it was gratifying in those days. Sir Bartle Frere, having heard about him, was desirous of meeting him, and asked him for an interview at the Government House. What transpired at the interview is not known.

A few months' later, an event of far-reaching importance took place in the life of Pherozeshah. The late Rustomji Jamsetjee Jejeebhoy, the second son of the first Parsi Baronet, and a man of remarkably enlightened views and catholic philanthropy, had offered in December 1863, a sum of Rs. 1,50,000 in trust "to enable five natives of India to proceed to England for the purpose of qualifying themselves for practice at the Bar in India."[2] The scholarships were to be open to a Parsi, a Hindu and a Portuguese in Bombay, and a Mohamedan and a Hindu, or East Indian from Calcutta or Madras, "all of good family connections, occupying a respectable position in society." The donor had further laid down that in making the selection, "the good moral character of the respective, parties must be an indispensable qualification, and not merely abilities alone." For each selected candidate the handsome provision of Rs. 30,000 was made, which included a sum of Rs. 10,000 to be presented to him on his qualifying himself as a barrister and producing a certificate of his good moral conduct during his residence in England. Such were the terms of the generous offer made by Rustomji Jamsetjee, a man whose charity was as wide and catholic as that of his illustrious father—as an instance of which might be mentioned his generous donation for the relief of Lancashire operatives at the time of the American Civil War—and who, it is related, had in the hey-day of his prosperity set apart the princely sum of Rs. 51 lacs for the benefit of the poor of his community. The downfall of this singularly enlightened and large-hearted citizen was one of the greatest tragedies of the Share Mania of 1865.

When applications were invited for the scholarship, Sir Alexander induced Pherozeshah to put forward his candidature, though his father had some misgivings about the propriety of his son accepting the benefit of a charitable trust, and wanted him to adopt a commercial career. Sir Alexander pointed out that it was in fact an honour to be selected as a candidate, and the elder Mehta gave in. It is interesting to note, as throwing a sidelight on the early conditions of Indian life, that not one Hindu came forward in Bombay to take the benefit of this magnificent provision. As Pherozeshah said some three years later in the course of a lecture before the East India Association, "the uneducated were withheld by the prejudices of caste and country, and the educated did not care to break abruptly some of the most sacred social and family ties, especially when the means of enlightenment were, to a certain extent, near at their hands."[3] In forwarding this gifted pupil's application, the eminent educationist wrote in terms of warm appreciation of his talents and character:

"I have great pleasure in testifying that Mr. Pherozeshah Merwany is in every way worthy of the benefaction which he seeks. He is on the whole the best student of all I have had to do with in the Elphinstone College. He has good abilities, industry, good sense, modesty, an excellent moral character, and remarkably gentlemanly and pleasing manners, From much association with him on the cricket field as well as in the lecture room, I can testify to his manliness and courage, which I think the committee will consider valuable qualifications. I beg you will lay before them this letter, and say to them with all respect that should their choice fall upon Mr. Pherozeshah Mehta, I should cordially congratulate the honourable founder of this benefaction on the worthy character of the young man selected to represent himself and the Parsee community in England."[4]

The choice of the committee happily fell upon Pherozeshah. In Calcutta the late W.C. Bonnerji was selected, and as Sir Alexander was going to England in December 1864, and was desirous of taking his pupil with him, the latter was allowed as a special grace to appear for his M.A. within six months of his passing the B.A. examination. The task was not an easy one, but those who knew him felt sure of his success. Their confidence was justified, and Pherozeshah became one of the first M.As. of the Bombay University. More exciting than the examination, however, was the prospect of his impending departure. He was going out to a new and wonderful world about which he had read and dreamt a great deal. The gifts with which he had been so amply endowed by Nature were to find the fullest scope for development, and the future seemed bright and full of hope. After weeks of preparation befitting the importance of the occasion, Pherozeshah sailed for England in December 1864. A visit to Europe was looked upon as a bit of an adventure in those days

It was some time before Pherozeshah settled down in his new surroundings. For a short while he stayed with Dadabhai Naoroji, who had gone to England as a partner in a prosperous firm of merchants, and was just embarking on his most remarkable political career. Afterwards, boarding arrangements were made with Professor Key, the Head Master of University College School and a Latin scholar of considerable reputation.

There were not many Indians in London at the time, but they were congenial spirits. Circumstanced as they were, they were thrown much into each other's society. Nonetheless, they moved about largely, and saw a great deal of the world around them. The dress that Pherozeshah and his immediate associates affected, though elegant, was a curious compromise between Western and Eastern ideas. A friend who saw them sailing down Oxford Street one day found them "very sprucely dressed up in the height of fashion, except that they had put on an oriental sort of head-drew-being dainty little black velvet caps, gay with long flowing blue silk tassels attached to a button fixed in the centre at the top, from which radiated some skeins of silk."[5] The head-gear was intended as a compliment to Dadabhai Naoroji, who exercised a great influence over the minds of the young Indians, and was a guide, philosopher and friend to them. Before he became a member of Parliament, he always went about in London plainly dressed in a long black broadcloth coat buttoned at the neck, and with his head covered by a black velvet cap with a small blue tassel. Pherozeshah and his companions had at first adopted this costume, but when yielding to the dictates of fashion, they dressed themselves up in the mode of the day, they retained the cap as a compliment to the guru. It was a somewhat outlandish combination, but it procured the young dandies a certain amount of attention which was by no means unacceptable.

Whilst in London, Pherozeshah was very friendly with Mr. and Mrs. D.D. Cama, at whose house he was a most welcome guest. Many Parsis in London gravitated to that delightful place in the country on Sundays, where, among other enjoyments, they were treated to a dinner cooked in the Parsi fashion. The typically Indian game of *chaupat* formed the principal amusement at these weekly gatherings. Pherozeshah was an adept at the game, in which the fun is apt to become faster and more furious, the more heavily one bangs the board with the pieces. So great were the excitement and noise round *chaupat* board that Cama's neighbour one day inquired why it was that he was always engaged on Sundays in hanging pictures! Pherozeshah was the outstanding figure at this and other gatherings. He took the lead in everything that was done, and his company looked to him for direction, as to one who was born to command. He was the arbiter elegantiarum, and his right to lay down the law was conceded without question. He was the most agreeable of companions, and his versatile talents, charm of manner and skill at various games assured him a warm welcome everywhere.

Apart from his legal studies, Pherozeshah devoted some time to the study of French, with which he soon picked up a fair acquaintance. He read a great deal of French Literature of the period of the Revolution, and was a warm admirer of Mirabeau and the other great actors in that earth-shaking drama. He was so fond of the language that on his return to India, when briefs were not too plentiful, he used to give lessons in French to some of his friends. As professional and public engagements began to multiply, he lost familiarity with the language, and during his subsequent visits to Europe never ventured to speak it.

Besides the company that has been mentioned, there were also about this time in London several Indians, who were destined to leave the impress of their personality on the country. They were gifted young men, and they made the most of their opportunities. Jamsetjee Tata, after many vicissitudes of fortune, lived to become a great captain of industry, and the pioneer of India's industrial awakening. Man Mohun Ghosh distinguished himself as a lawyer and politician during the comparatively short span of life that was allotted to him. Budrudin Tyabji enjoyed an immense practice at the Bar, rose to the Bench, and carried with him there the qualities which had given him an honoured place among the leaders of the people. W.C. Bonnerji became a lawyer and a leader of unquestioned eminence, and his massive personality lent distinction to the public life of Bengal. All these young men used to meet at Dadabhai's place, where Pherozeshah came closely in contact with them. This intimate association was of considerable value to him, and laid in the case of Bonnerji, the foundations of a political friendship, which was of the greatest benefit to India in the days when they and other devoted patriots strove to implant in her the seeds of new ideas, and the impulse towards a higher life.

The inner circle of Pherozeshah's friends made good also. Hormasji Wadya prospered in Kathiawar, did useful public service and achieved a Knighthood. C.M. Cursetjee, after a period of service in the mofussil, became a judge of the Presidency Small Causes Court. Limji Banaji rose by slow degrees to the responsible position of prothonotary of the High Court. Jamsetjee Cama, confirmed *bon vivant,* prospered sufficiently as a solicitor to enable him to indulge his inordinate fondness for the good things of life. None indeed of that promising little group failed to make good.

Though Pherozeshah was thrown largely in the society of his own countrymen, it must not be imagined that he moved in a narrow circle. The Indian student was a bit of a rarity in those days, and was not regarded as a nuisance or an object of suspicion, as he became at a later period. The doors of English society were not closed to him, and he was received with warmth and kindness in many a home. Pherozeshah had thus no difficulty in making friends amongst people of good social standing. Among others, he met the Reverend Long, well-known in connection with the indigo trouble in the sixties. Through the kindness of the latter, he had opportunities of meeting Lord Shaftesbury, the Father of factory legislation, the Duke of Argyle, Secretary of State for India, and other notable men.[6]

It was a memorable epoch in the history of England and the world. Carlyle, Ruskin, Mill, Darwin, Herbert Spencer—to mention only a few of the great teachers of the age—delivered their message, and humanity felt profoundly shaken in its beliefs, ideas and dogmas. "Mazzini and Victor Hugo imparted activity, elevation and the generous breadth of cosmopolitan outlook to the most ardent spirits of the new time in our own island." In politics, Liberalism made its appearance as a stimulating and powerful factor in national progress. Cobden and Bright and Gladstone breathed a new spirit into the political controversies of the day. Across the Atlantic, "humanity fought one of its most glorious battles," and the curse of slavery was put an end to. A revolution was sweeping over men's thoughts and ideas, and in the words of Lord Morley, "only those whose minds are numbed by the suspicion that all times are tolerably alike, and men and women much of a muchness, will deny that it was a generation of intrepid effort forward."[7]

It was in such an atmosphere that Pherozeshah imbibed those principles which ever afterwards governed his public career. Contact with all that was healthy in Western life and thought instilled into him a breadth of view, courage, independence of thought and a love of ordered progress, allied with a certain conservatism which lies at the root of the British character. He developed early those traits which raised him so greatly above his countrymen, and displayed a maturity of thought which impressed all who came in contact with him. He took a keen interest in the problems of the day, particularly as they affected his country, and was one of the most active members of the East India Association, which was founded by Dadabhai Naoroji in October 1866, "for the independent and disinterested advocacy and promotion by all legitimate means of the interest and welfare of India generally."[8] The Association owed its existence to the support of many enlightened Indian princes, which Dadabhai was able to secure for it on his return to India for a brief period after the commercial crash which had involved among others the firm of which he was a partner. The organization, until it was captured by retired Anglo-Indian officials, did yeoman service in stimulating political activity among Indians and educating English opinion about the problems of India. Its annual reports contain a treasure-house of information on a multitude of subjects, and may be read with profit even at the present day.

Before this Association, Pherozeshah read a paper on *The Educational System in the Presidency of Bombay,* which evoked warm praise from a small but appreciative audience. It was characterized as an "able, clever and elaborate paper,"[9] and the young lecturer was asked to embody his views in a series of resolutions to be brought up again for discussion.

After defining the true aims of Indian education, Pherozeshah went on to express his conviction that for a long time to come elementary education of the masses must give place to a high liberal education. True, the latter would be confined to a handful of men, but he declared that the history of every great movement in the progress of civilization, end of all the reformations and revolutions showed that it is these few men who do the work of the uplifting of the masses, and who, endowed with real earnestness, deep thought and comprehensive insight, create and mould the new ideas, and transfer them thus ready-made to the multitude, to be received by them on their authority and example. To this view he clung with tenacity throughout his long career. Equally strong was his conviction that the vernaculars of the country were unsuited to become the vehicles of a liberal education, and that English ought consequently to be the principal medium of imparting knowledge. The controversies which centred round such questions in those days cannot be said to have lost their interest even at the present moment. To those seeking illumination on the subject, the lecture with its mass of facts and arguments presents much that may be pondered over with profit.

This was not Pherozeshah's only incursion into the controversies of the day. He took an active and intelligent interest in various public questions, which enabled those who came in contact with him to understand and appreciate his gifted personality. Among those who formed a high opinion of his capacity was Professor Key, who in 1868 wrote to Pherozeshah in terms of generous appreciation such as may well have flattered the latter. "Already entertaining a very high opinion of your race in general," wrote the great Latinist, "I must say without flattery that I found in you something exceeding all my expectations; and I look forward to your playing an important part in India, especially in procuring for the Parsees, and I hope the

Hindoos also, as well as others, a status in society more worthy of them. Keep this grand object in view, and do your best to attain eminence at the Bombay Bar, for I feel sure you have qualities, both natural and acquired, that may enable you to do so."

This was on the eve of Pherozeshah's departure from England. He had been called to the Bar in Easter Term in 1868 and had been received at the Benchers' Table. A bill for £ 1-1s. made out by "John Punt, second butler," for proportionate contribution to the expenses of a wine party affords evidence that the occasion was duly celebrated. As he had completed his training, his father was desirous that he should return at the earliest opportunity, preferably with Sir Alexander, who was coming out in July. The failure of Rustumji Jamsetjee, shortly after Pherozeshah's departure for England, had deprived the latter of the benefit of the scholarship, and had thrown on the elder Mehta a burden of which he was anxious to be relieved. His son with his extravagant habits had spent quite a small fortune during his three and a half years' stay in England. Pherozeshah delayed his departure, however, as he wanted to give a few finishing touches to his education. Ultimately, with the good wishes of those who were taking a sympathetic interest in his career, and to the regret of his intimate associates, who felt that life was losing much of its savour by his departure, Pherozeshah sailed for India in September 1868. Those four years which he had spent in England had been among the happiest in his life, and had equipped him with much that went to the making of his remarkable public career.

On the way out, Pherozeshah made an acquaintance with an Englishman occupying high office in India–William Wedderburn (as he then was), one of the most earnest and disinterested champions of its interests that this country has ever known. Through the good offices of the latter, the young barrister was on his return made a justice of the Peace, and thus given an early opportunity of acquainting himself with the municipal affairs of the city, which were then vested in the hands of the Bench of justices.

On the very afternoon of his arrival, Pherozeshah attended a function which had a peculiar interest for him. It was held at the Framji Cowasji Institute, where a large and distinguished company had gathered under the chairmanship of Sir Richard Couch, Chief Justice of Bombay, to bid farewell to Sir Alexander Grant, who was retiring from the country to take up the appointment of Principal of the Edinburgh University, which some years before, he had sought to obtain, but without success. The latter was glad to get an opportunity of meeting his young friend whom he greeted as one who had come back, "fresh with the legal atmosphere of Lincoln's Inn upon him." The address, which was numerously signed by his friends and pupils, testified to the warm regard and affection in which Grant was held by all classes of people. By his devoted labours in what was almost a virgin field, he had deserved well of the City and the Presidency. The history of education in Western India contains the names of many distinguished men, but none greater than that of the gifted translator of the Ethics of Aristotle, who, in the early sixties, moulded the lives and thoughts of a generation eager to learn and to spread the light of education far and wide in the land.

Pherozeshah lost no time in settling down to the work of his profession. He rented chambers in a somewhat ricketty old house in Apollo Street, where the inevitable period of waiting for briefs that seemed a long time in coming was enlivened by the excellent company that gathered there every afternoon after the day's work was over. In those days, the High Court was located in a building occupied later by the Great Western Hotel. The Appellate Court with its various establishments was at Mazagon. At the head of the Judiciary was Sir Richard Couch, an eminent judge, who was supported by able colleagues, and by a Bar which included that eccentric genius T.C. Anstey.

The little group of briefless juniors, which spent its time mostly in the corridor or the common room, had an uphill task before it. It is true the profession was not over-crowded, and competition in the sense in which it is understood now did not exist. But the entire practice was more or less concentrated in the hands of a few eminent counsel, such as Anstey, Scoble, Green, Latham, White, Mariott, and one or two others. It was a very difficult thing either to dislodge them from their position, or even to carry away a few crumbs from their richly-laden table. Compared with the Bar of the present day, these contemporaries of Pherozeshah might be regarded as veritable giants. The litigant public ran after them, and took no notice of the knot of hapless juniors hungrily looking for briefs. Badrudin Tyabji, son of an enterprising Borah merchant, and the first Indian to join the Bombay Bar, was, perhaps, the earliest to make his way up. He had the backing of his brother Curnrudin, who was the first Indian solicitor. Shantaram Narayen and Nanabhai Haridas also commanded some practice, but it was on the appellate side. There were hardly any firms of Indian attorneys to give the young men a lift in the profession. A deal of patronage rested in the hands of managing clerks, whose smile was to be counted, and some of whom were as important figures as the solicitors whom they served.

The indifference of attorneys and the haughtiness of seniors did not, however, weigh on the spirits of the gay little coterie that daily met in Pherozeshah's chambers. They were spirited young men, full of the *joie de vivre*, and they divided their time between tea parties, political discussions and practical jokes. One of the unwritten rules of the company was that each newcomer on his arrival was to entertain his colleagues to dinner. These functions were usually held in a private room at Old Pallonji's Adelphi Hotel, situated at Byculla, which was then a fashionable locality. It was the first hotel in Bombay worth the name, and through the personality of its old proprietor, familiar to hosts of Englishmen and Indians in all parts of the Presidency, it had come to be regarded as an institution. The dinners were highly popular and promoted friendly intercourse. One of the newcomers, Homi Bennett, contrived to avoid the function, however. A citation on a printed form obtained from the Sheriffs office, and drawn up in all the ponderous legal phraseology was issued, requiring the culprit to appear "at the bar of the Dinner Tribunal, coram Pherozeshah Mehta," to show cause why he should not be put out of caste. A court-peon was got to serve the rule on him, as he sat one afternoon in one of the courts, whilst the "Tribunal" awaited results in the common-room. They had not long to wait. Following on the service of the citation, the newcomer who was of a very irascible temperament, and unable to appreciate a joke, rushed up in a towering rage, made straight for Pherozeshah, caught hold of him, and threatened to throw him out of one of the windows overlooking the old ice-house, one of the landmarks of Bombay that has recently disappeared. Prompt and vigorous intervention prevented a fight, however, and harmony was ultimately restored by the delinquent offering reparation in the shape of a modest lunch washed down with a hock-cup. Those were happy days indeed. In later years men saw much of Pherozeshah at various places, at the Ripon Club, the Presidency Association and the chambers at Esplanade Road which became a regular salon. They found him courteous, affable and full of genial humour. But nowhere did he give such play to his fancies and ready wit as he used to do in that choice circle of early friends, full of hopes and ambitions of youth.

With the removal of the Court to the imposing pile of buildings on the Oval, the little group dispersed in various directions. Badrudin Tyabji got lost in the ever-increasing volume of briefs; H.A. Wadya winged his way to Rajkot to earn wealth and fame, Limji Banaji accepted a subordinate position in the High Court; C.M. Cursetjee got absorbed in the mofussil judiciary; Dady Cama returned to London to take charge of his father's business; Bal Mangesh Wagle went to Baroda, as Chief Judge in the wake of Dadabhai Naoroji who was appointed prime minister of the Gaekwad; and poor Bennett developed homicidal mania and committed suicide. One by one they all disappeared, some to meet again under different circumstances, and in different surroundings. As one who cherished vivid recollections of those unforgettable days wrote, "crowds indeed have since come and gone and filled Pherozeshah's chambers, but never did the flavour and fragrance of the familiar intercourse of the old circle of those happy early days return; other times succeeded, and other men and manners."[11]

The time during which Pherozeshah had to cool his heels was not wasted by him. He was very regular in his attendance in the various courts, and assiduous in his study of text-books and reports. He attracted to himself the favourable notice of justices Westropp, and Bailey, the latter of whom was very sympathetic and hospitable to the little contingent of Indian barristers. Off the Court, Pherozeshah amused himself by writing in various journals, including *The Indian Statesman*, a paper founded by that "Bayard of Indian Journalism," Robert Knight. He set himself up occasionally as a dramatic critic, being fond of the theatre, and once invited on himself a very scurrilous attack from one of the outraged dramatists whom he had criticized. With the aid of Dady Patel, a scion of a very respectable family, with whom theatricals were an obsession, he stage-managed several amateur performances and got up in aid of local charities.

By slow degrees, work began to flow in the direction of Pherozeshah and his friends. The atmosphere which surrounded the young men began to be less frigid, as gradually Anstey, Mariott, Macpherson, Scoble and others showed themselves friendly to them. The process of climbing up was, nevertheless, somewhat slow, and in the struggle several gave up practice at the Bar, and succumbed to the little temptations that were held out to them. In this way, some of the close and constant companions of Pherozeshah were snapped up, and the Bar knew them no more. From the first, Pherozeshah, confident in his abilities, had determined not to be turned aside by any considerations whatsoever from the pursuit of his profession. As he himself once said at a gathering in his honour, "an eminent member of Government, a most broad-minded man and a man of high liberal culture," had sent for him very shortly after his return from England, and offered to appoint him as a First Class Sub-judge. It was a problem for him, for briefs were not too frequently coming in those days, and as his friends reminded him, his income just enabled him to go to a restaurant occasionally. But he declined the offer, and there is no doubt that the chief reason which prompted his action was his desire to preserve his independence, and to keep himself free to serve the public interest, which was always close to his heart.

Pherozeshah's confidence in himself was ultimately justified, for his abilities, powers of exposition, and skill in cross-examination began to compel recognition, and attorneys started taking notice of the promising young counsel. One of the earliest cases which brought him into prominence was the celebrated Parsi Towers of Silence case, which excited public interest for weeks on end. He had the good fortune to be Anstey's junior in that case. That remarkable man, though not very pleased at first with the idea of having an inexperienced Indian briefed with him, soon came to form a high opinion of Pherozeshah, though he could not quite reconcile himself to the latter's massive turban! In Anstey's opinion, publicly expressed, his brilliant junior had "all the germs of future eminence in him."[12]

But it was, after all, mofussil practice that laid the foundations of Pherozeshah's remarkable success at the Bar. From an early period, Gujarat and Kathiawar began to requisition the services of the young lawyer, who had the habit of giving his opponents an uncomfortable time, and who stood no nonsense from even the most arbitrary judge or magistrate. The Surat Riot case, which gave way to the introduction of the Licence Tax in the seventies, securely established the reputation he was making, and placed him at once in the front rank of mofussil practitioners. The ability, resourcefulness, and forensic eloquence which he displayed in the case made his name famous throughout Gujarat, and briefs began to pour in from of all quarters. That settled the direction of his professional career, which thereafter lay largely in the mofussil, though, if he had chosen to, he could have commanded an extensive practice in Bombay, where clients were no less eager to engage his services. But with his growing public engagements, it suited him to cultivate mofussil practice, which was by no means as exacting as work in the High Court, and was equally lucrative.

His professional engagements took him to all parts of the Presidency, and familiarized him with the modes and habits of life and thought of people of all conditions. Facilities for travel and accommodation were very inadequate in those days, when the railway had not penetrated to all parts of the country, and a good deal of roughing had to be done, to which Pherozeshah, who had not developed the extreme fastidiousness of his later years, readily submitted. Among other places, he went sometimes to the Chief Commissioner's Court at Mount Abu. The journey had to be made from Ahmedabad, via Deesa, in a *dumni* cart drawn by bullocks. In the hot season, the intense heat of the scorching plains of Rajputana made travelling by day very uncomfortable; so the *dumni* used to roll on all the night, discharging its burden at some indifferent rest-house or dak bungalow, where the day was spent in rest and sleep.

Discomfort and fatigue, however, made no difference to Pherozeshah's habits. He always had his bath in the morning and, scrupulously performed his toilet, which was a somewhat elaborate affair even in those days. It gave him a good appetite for breakfast, which he enjoyed despite the heat and tedium of the journey. The only thing he disliked was physical exertion, which after his college days, he carefully avoided.

The atmosphere in which Pherozeshah moved was stimulating in many ways; it gave tone to his character and mental attitude. The Bar in his time was energetic, and zealous of its rights and privileges. In 1871, when the Indian Evidence Act was on the anvil, it sent across a strong protest to the then Viceroy, the Earl of Mayo, against some of the provisions of the Bill, which by implication cast a reflection on the integrity and independence of the legal profession in India. The distinguished jurist who drafted the Act, Sir James Fitz James Stephen, though complained of the uncompromising vigour of the strictures of the Bombay Bar, thought it prudent, however, to drop the objectionable clauses.

In 1872, he became a member of the Corporation of Bombay and was thrice elected its Chairman. In the Bombay Corporation he showed keen interest in the problem of drainage, primary education, medical relief, the apportionment of police charges, water supply etc. He took a leading part in the Ilbert Bill agitation. Along with Dadabhai and Ranade, he was one of the founders of the Indian National Congress. Along with Telang and Badruddin Tayabji he founded the Bombay Presidency Association in 1885, which expressed its opinion on political matters. He had a tremendous command over legal literature and made a name for himself as a lawyer, as a member of the Bombay Corporation and as a senator of the University of Bombay.

He was appointed a member of the Bombay Legislative Council by Lord Reay. He was a member of the Bombay in 1886. In 1892, he was elected to Legislative Council for fifteen years. In the Bombay Legislative Council, Pherozeshah expressed himself with great force and independence on questions of financial statement, agriculturists' relief, import duties, Police Act amendment, Contagious Diseases Act etc. He pointed out the perils to Indian finance from frontier wars, the unequal distribution of Home military charges, the growth of Military Expenditure and Exchange Compensation Allowances. For three years he was a member of the Indian Legislative Council (1894-1897). He was noted for his vigorous and brilliant elocution and his fearlessness. He was a dialectician, a master of biting and caustic sarcasm and satire, and a splendid politician.[13]

Pherozeshah had a dominating personality and for many years he almost controlled the Congress. He was the President of the Indian National Congress in 1890. He was the president of the Bombay Provincial Conference held at Poona in 1892. He was the Chairman of the Reception Committee of the Indian National Congress in 1889 and again in 1904. In his speech, in 1904, at Bombay he repeated the significance of the divinely ordained British connexion with India. In the historic split at Surat in 1907 Pherozeshah and Gokhale were the key-figures in the Moderate camp. It was due to their initiative that the venue of the Congress had been shifted to Surat from Nagpur. Pherozeshah was elected the Chairman of the Indian National Congress again in 1910 but due to some undeclared reason he tendered his resignation.[14]

An ardent lover of progress and liberty, Pherozeshah was strongly conservative in his outlook on some of the problems of the day. The love of ordered progress which his well-balanced mind and early training instilled into him made him averse to all violent or sudden changes. Deeply imbued with the teaching of English History, he had a profound reverence for constitutional forms and an abiding faith in the virtue of gradual and peaceful evolution of 'freedom slowly broadening down from precedent to precedent.'[15]

Always making the most of what he got, even if, as invariably happened, it fell short of what he had fought for, he set himself immediately to prepare for the next advance. He did not worry about the distant goal but strove for what he thought the country was prepared for and had a right to demand, never doubting it would achieve its destiny in the process of time.

Pherozeshah was far and away the greatest political leader India had known. He never appealed to the masses as did Dadabhai Naoroji or Tilak, for instance. His hold was mainly over the educated and thinking section of the people. His impressive presence, personality and the power of his mind dominated all who worked with him or followed his lead. As was observed of Gladstone, when he spoke, he uplifted debate from whatever rut of mediocrity it may have fallen into. That was the power of this orator. When he sat silent, his mere presence communicated to the House a sense of dignity and a moral strength, easier to feel than to describe. That was the quality of the man.

It was remarkable how the many gifted men with whom Pherozeshah was associated in various spheres of public life allowed their will and judgement to be subordinated to him. The wail of the Punjab delegate that his personality dominated everybody faithfully, represented the feelings of those who often differed from him, and yet found themselves helpless in his presence.

This supremacy becomes all the more remarkable when we think of the men over whom it was exercised. There were some who were in no way inferior to Pherozeshah in vigour of intellect; there were others who closely rivalled him in gifts of speech and independence of character. There was none, however, who combined in him so many of the qualities which compel the admiration and command the allegiance of one's fellowmen; and in that, apart from that undefinable called 'personality', must be found an explanation of Pherozeshah's dominance over all who came in contact with him.

There were men who in his later days made comparisons between him and Gokhale. Nothing could have been more foolish. The truth is that each did work complementary to that of the other, including and what the other was probably not capable of accomplishing. Gokhale certainly could not have roused as much as Pherozeshah did the intelligentsia of the country from the apathy and even hostility with which a large section regarded the national movement. Gokhale could not have stood up as resolutely and as courageously as Pherozeshah did against injustice, oppression or autocracy. On the other hand, Pherozeshah was temperamentally incapable of the active and sustained educative work which Gokhale did from day to day, and the propaganda he carried on both in England and in India, and which owed its success as much to his high character as to his attainments. Comparisons between two such men are meaningless. Each was great in his own sphere, and together they made a portable contribution to the building up of the New India of which Dadabhai Naoroji had laid the foundations.[16]

REFERENCES

1. Mody, Homi, *Sir Pherozeshah Mehta* (Bombay: Asia Publishing House), 1963, pp. 3-4.
2. *Ibid.*, p. 5.
3. *Ibid.*
4. *Ibid.*, pp. 5-6.
5. Chintamani, C.Y., *Speeches and Writings of Sir Pherozeshah Mehta* (Allahabad: *The Indian Press*), 1905, p. 2.
6. *Ibid.*, p. 36.
7. *Ibid.*
8. Naoroji, Dadabhai, *Poverty and Un-British Rule in India* (New Delhi: Publications Division, Government of India, Ministry of Information and Broadcasting), 1962, p. 17.
9. Mody, Homi, *Sir Pherozeshah Mehta, op. cit.*, p. 12.
10. *Ibid.*, p. 13.
11. *Ibid.* p. 18.
12. Sastri, V. S. Srinivasa, *Life and Times of Sir Pherozeshah Mehta* (Bangalore: Bangalore Printing Co.), 1937, p. 9.
13. Varma, V. P., *Modern Indian Political Thought* (Agra: Lakshmi Narain Agarwal), 1961, p. 166.
14. *Ibid.*
15. Mody, Homi, *Pherozeshah Mehta* (New Delhi: Publications Division, Ministry of Information and Broadcasting, Government of India), 1963, p. 186.
16. *Ibid.*, p. 187.

2

IDEOLOGY AND PERCEPTION

Though his circumstances and habits of life made it necessary for Pherozeshah to build up a substantial income, from his youth he had determined to devote himself to public affairs. It was not long after his return from England that he was admitted to the ranks of those who were striving to infuse political activity into a city more or less absorbed in the pursuit of commerce and industry. At a public meeting held in Bombay under the chairmanship of Sir Jamsetjee Jejeebhoy, second Baronet of that name, the Bombay Branch of the East India Association was launched into existence amidst considerable enthusiasm. The Bombay Association, which had as its secretary that rugged and sternly independent publicist, Naoroji Furdunji, who was known as "the tribune of the people," had done useful work in championing Indian interests, but had ceased for some time to be an active political force. In the words of its founder, Dadabhai Naoroji, it was to act simply as a messenger and an agent of the parent institution. After years, when the latter ceased to represent the ideas and ambitions of its early founders, the possession of the funds of the Bombay Branch became the subject of a bitter controversy, which arose out of the character of agency stamped upon it on its foundation.

Pherozeshah and Bal Mangesh Wagle were appointed the first secretaries of the new Association. In moving their appointment, one of the speakers referred to them as young lawyers and distinguished graduates of the University, and hoped that "they would not allow their youthful enthusiasm to cool down when briefs began to accumulate upon their hands."[1] The suggestion underlying this remark was not unnatural. Too often have the prizes of a professional career succeeded in withdrawing some of our best intellects from the arena of public life. But little did the speaker realize that atleast in one of the youthful secretaries, there dwelt a public spirit which was no less remarkable than the talents which he so freely devoted to the service of his country.

The first public activity of the new recruit to the ranks of political workers was in the direction of organizing a testimonial to Dadabhai Naoroji in recognition of the eminent services he was rendering to India. The Grand Old Man was then in the early stages of a career, whose inspiration was to touch an ever widening circle and to witness at its culmination the triumph of the principles which were the mainsprings of its activities for more than half a century. The people of India already recognized in him an unflinching champion of their interests, and the testimonial got up by the citizens of Bombay was but one of the many proofs of their confidence and regard. To the pleasant task of making it worthy of the recipient, Pherozeshah applied himself with energy, his labour and those of others, backed by an enthusiastic public, which resulted in the collection of a handsome amount. This was presented as a purse to Dadabhai in July 1869, at a meeting largely attended by all classes and communities, and which might be regarded as the first representative gathering of the citizens of Bombay. It was entirely characteristic of the man that though he was poor, he dedicated the entire sum to the furtherance of the causes which were so dear to his heart.[2]

In December 1869, Pherozeshah delivered a lecture before the Bombay Branch of the East India Association on the Grant-in-Aid system in Bombay. In his paper before the parent body in London, he had taken a general survey of the position of education as it stood at the time. He had dealt briefly with the Grant-in-Aid system and condemned it. The present lecture was devoted to a more exhaustive treatment of the subject, and was directed towards showing that the policy of the Government had been largely responsible for the slow progress which education had made in India. After pointing out that whatever success the Grant-in-Aid system had achieved in England was due to the widespread perception of the general and special advantages of education, the existence of a richly-endowed set of colleges and grammar schools and the necessity for the recognition of a denominational system of education, the lecture proceeded to show that these conditions did not exist in India. He was of the opinion that the framers of the famous Despatch of 1854 had set too great a store by the growing appetite which the richer classes were supposed to feel for the acquisition of knowledge. Such, however, was not the case. Nor were the Directors right in thinking that the system was likely to foster a spirit of self-reliance which was of great importance for the well-being of a nation. In Pherozeshah's opinion, nothing was more calculated "to induce the instinct of self-government than a thorough liberal education of a high order," and it was better at once to establish a full-blown educational system which would give an impetus to the movement towards self-government, than to adopt a system which would achieve that end by a slow and laborious process. As to the ways and means, the lecturer suggested:

"In the first place, the State should establish such a framework of a complete co-ordinated system of primary schools, secondary schools, or, as we call them High schools, Normal schools, general and technical colleges and universities, as, without being too elaborate, might be capable of expansion and development with the progress of the times; and secondly, that whenever in educational institution, say a High school, could be established in a certain locality, the Government should set about directly to supply the want with private, local and other aid if it was forthcoming, without waiting for it if it was not, and further that it should do so in a thoroughly efficient manner, without leaving it unprovided in any essential particular."[3]

The lecture then dealt with the question of expenditure, and concluded with a brief survey of what European countries had done in the cause of education. The discussion that followed was interesting. Ranade took exception to the strictures which had been passed on the Board of Directors, who, in his opinion, had certainly not erred in their magnificent conception of a national scheme of education, suited to the circumstances of India at the time, and towards whom it behoved them all to assume a most respectful tone. As for the Grant-in-Aid system, it had worked very well, and in any case it was too early to sit in judgement upon it. It was obvious that Government with the assistance of private liberality or enterprise must accomplish greater results than a pure Government agency could hope to achieve. Bal Mangesh Wagle defended Pherozeshah against these criticisms, and in support of the view advanced in the lecture that the richer classes had not yet begun to appreciate the advantages of education, gave the instance of a boy who wanted from him a certificate of poverty to enable him to be admitted as a free student in the Elphinstone College, and on whose marriage only a month before Rs. 5,000 had been spent by his parents! Wedderburn, who was present, stated that whatever might be thought of the question of higher education being subsidized, there was no doubt that it was the duty of the State to provide primary education for the masses, and the system at work appeared to be well adapted to secure the end in view. The general opinion as expressed at the meeting seemed to be that the Grant-in-Aid system had not worked badly.

The policy of the Government in the matter of education has not been marked by imagination or statesmanship will be conceded by most people. At the farewell gathering already referred to, on the eve of Sir Alexander Grant's retirement from the country, he spoke with bitterness of the one per cent devoted to the cause of education, science and art, and observed with much force, "when we consider the 40 per cent devoted to the military department we must, I think, consider that it is somewhat surprising that people should be heard boasting that it is the pride and duty and mission of England to educate the people of India, when such a wretched pittance as this is all that is given for the advancement and spread of education."[4] The Despatch of 1854 had breathed a spirit of genuine liberality, and had grandly conceived the scope and purpose of education for the people of India. Normally developed, the policy outlined by the Despatch would have borne results worthy of its framers. But the Mutiny of 1857 rudely upset the balance of mind of many Englishmen, and induced a different outlook altogether. That high-minded Englishman, Allan Octavian Hume, who later became the Father of the Congress, complained at the time that "many entirely disapprove of any efforts to cultivate the native mind, many condemn as unconditionally a merely secular education." Sixty years have since rolled by, and yet who can say that the old prejudices against education have died away? There are signs, however, that more enlightened views on the subject are beginning to prevail, and the responsibility of the State on which Pherozeshah laid such emphasis, is coming to be more widely recognized.

About this time, public attention was focused on a controversy which has dragged on for more than half a century. The question of the larger admission of Indians into the ranks of the Covenanted Service has occupied the foremost place among the political problems of this country. The Act of 1833 laid down in emphatic terms the principle of equality, and declared that "no native of the said territories, nor any natural-born subject of His Majesty resident therein, shall, by reason only of his religion, place of birth, descent, colour, or any of them, be disabled from holding any place, office or employment under the said Company." The question was earnestly considered at the time of this declaration, and sympathy towards the legitimate ambitions and aspirations of Indians was expressed by Sir Robert Peel, Lord Lansdowne and other British statesmen. The subject came again to the fore in 1853, and among the measures suggested for introducing a larger Indian element in the administration was a proposal for holding simultaneous examinations in England and in India. A departmental committee of the Indian Office accordingly went into the question in 1860, and declared that it was not only just but expedient that the natives of India should be employed in the administration of India to as large an extent as possible, consistently with the maintenance of British supremacy. After observing that no positive disqualification of Indians existed even at that time, the Committee went on to say:

"Practically however they are excluded. The law declares them eligible, but the difficulties opposed to a native living in India and residing in England for a time are so great that, as a general rule, it is almost impossible for a native successfully to compete at the periodical examinations held in England. Were this inequality removed, we should no longer be exposed to the charge of making promise to the ear, and breaking it to the heart."[5]

After discussing the schemes that had been proposed to remedy the existing inequality, the Committee unhesitatingly declared itself in favour of simultaneous examinations "as being the fairest and most in accordance with the principles of a general competition for a common object." Such was the considered opinion of a body whose competence or impartiality could not be challenged. Needless to say, however, nothing was done, and the question after being continuously agitated for over half a century has now ceased to possess any interest whatever for the people of this country. In the sixties, however, hopes ran high, and the energy and enthusiasm of Dadabhai Naoroji, and the youthful band which followed his lead, kept the question prominently before the public. In August 1867, Dadabhai read a paper before the East India Association advocating that competitive examinations should take place in India for a portion of the appointments to the Civil Service. An interesting discussion ensued, and it was resolved to submit a memorial to the Secretary of State for India.[6] A deputation from the Association accordingly waited upon Sir Stafford Northcote, who expressed himself favourably with regard to the changes proposed, and stated that he was in correspondence with Sir John Lawrence and others in India on the subject. A year later, Dadabhai read another paper before the Association, dealing with the thoroughness, characteristic of him, with all the objections urged against the suggestions contained in the memorial. The immediate object of the paper was to support the following motion of Fawcett in the House of Commons[7]:

"That this House whilst cordially approving of the system of open competition for appointments in the East India Civil Service, is of opinion that the people of India have not a fair chance of competing for these appointments as long as the examinations are held nowhere but in London; this House would then deem it desirable that simultaneously with the examination in London, the same examination should be held in Calcutta, Bombay and Madras."

The end of it all was the introduction by Sir Stafford Northcote of the East India Bill, clause 6 which empowered the authorities in India to appoint Indians to any office, place or employment, even though they had not been admitted to the Civil Service of Her Majesty in India. In other words, instead of the principle of competition upon equal terms which was demanded, a principle of selection was introduced, which could not but be arbitrary in its working, let alone its other objectionable features.

The Bill had a somewhat mixed reception. Some people were disappointed that the scheme of simultaneous examinations had found no place in it, while others were willing to recognize the good intentions of the Secretary of State and discover in the Bill the first measure of fulfilment of the legitimate aspirations of Indians to share in the governance of their country. Among the latter was Dadabhai, who, in a paper, forwarded from Bombay, where he then was, to the East India Association, took up an attitude of hopefulness and a desire to give the scheme a trial. This optimism, it is interesting to note, does not appear to have been shared by some of his young disciples, for in 1870 we find Pherozeshah vigorously attacking the proposals outlined in the Bill. In a paper read before the Bombay Branch on the 27th April 1870, he entered upon a spirited defence of the competitive system, winding up his argument with a long quotation from Macaulay, who at the close of a striking passage in one of his speeches in the House of Commons on the occasion of the passing of the Act of 1853—when the Civil Service was first thrown open to competition—had laid down the general conclusion that those men who distinguished themselves most in academical competition when they were young, were those who after years distinguished themselves most in the competition of life.

Pherozeshah regarded the competitive system as infinitely superior as a test of qualification to appointment by selection, which he condemned as opening the door to jobbery of the worst character, and as being unjust and demoralising to the Indians whom it was intended to benefit. He could not understand how anyone could fail to perceive the relative value of the two systems, and he felt that there was some silent reason operating on the minds of the framers of the measure. He could not help thinking that they must have been led away by the specious argument that intellectual cultivation did not induce moral cultivation. This belief has been general, and has found expression in a variety of ways and been largely exploited for political ends; and those who have followed the educational policy of the last few years cannot fail to have been struck by the retrograde tendency which has manifested itself in several directions. At the beginning, however, the question was free from the political taint which has so largely dominated the consideration of it at the present day. A striking passage in Pherozeshah's paper, which will bear extensive quotation, deals with these insidious attacks on "literary" education, which have become such a fashion in recent years:

If we took those periods in the development of a society when morality did not exist separately, but was still absorbed in religion, it would be perfectly true to say that intellectual culture did not teach morality. Thus, during the early ages of Christianity what even intellectual training there was, would have been utterly insufficient to form the morals of its pupils. In those days nothing could have performed that task so well and so thoroughly as a religious education. History abounds with instances of such periods. There was a time when Judaism possessed its sole and best culture in the Mosaic books. There was a time when Hellenism had to look only to the theological poems of such men as Homèr and Hesiod; there was a time when Mohamedanism depended for its civilization on the Koran alone. The next stage, however, of the progress of these societies, if they succeed in advancing to it, is one in which morality emancipates itself from religious shackles and appears under other shapes and other forms. Such has been the case with English in common with all Western civilizations. The Apostles and the Fathers are now superseded by Poets and Historians and Philosophers. Not that these people have taken to preaching and inculcating directly and indirectly the moral precepts once contained in the Bible and its Commentaries. The transformation takes place in a less demonstrative manner. The religious teaching slowly distributes itself in the shape of moral axioms and ideas, which in their transition instil themselves into the mind as its first principles. These first principles are influenced by all your thoughts, actions and utterances. The Poet, the Historian, the Philosopher cannot sing or write but on the condition of remaining true to this heritage which they receive. And once you have a complete literature so thoroughly and unconsciously imbued with the highest moral teaching of the day, then religion has done its peculiar work, and intellectual education coincides with moral cultivation.[8]

At the close of the lecture several resolutions were passed which condemned the Bill as likely to lead to the perpetration of political jobbery, and not calculated to open the doors of the Civil Service to Indians in the most honourable manner, in the words of Macaulay, "by conquest, as a matter of right, and not as a mere elementary donation." The meeting was further of opinion that "the natives of India while protesting against exceptional obstructions which are not shared generally, are, however, ambitious of obtaining admission to the Civil Service of their country in a fair fight and open competition."[9]

Despite all this agitation, the Bill became law as it stood. It may be stated here that little was done under the Act till 1879, when rules were framed by which one-sixth of the posts reserved for the Covenanted Service were to be ultimately set apart for Indians; and for gradually carrying out this intention, the number of posts thrown open for competition in England in 1880 was reduced accordingly. It will be seen at once how inadequately this scheme fulfilled the hopes and aspirations which had been aroused. In 1870, when the Act was passed, there were only nine Indians holding the higher appointments. Within the next 20 years, sixty more Indians were able to get themselves appointed as "Statutory Civilians" under the rules. Such was the measure of fulfilment of the promises held out at the time. Even Lord Lytton had to admit, in a secret report to the authorities in England, that the people of the country had been "cheated" of their hopes.

The Statutory Civilians had a somewhat short and ignoble career. Their recruitment justified in the main the criticisms of those who had condemned the system, and an outcry was raised for its abandonment. A Commission was appointed in 1886, "to devise scheme which might reasonably be hoped to possess the necessary elements of finality, and to do full justice to the claims of natives of India to higher employment in the public service."

The qualities which placed Pherozeshah in the forefront of Indian politicians also brought him to the front rank in his profession. Courage, independence and skill in argument are naturally as much prized by parties to litigation as by the general public. The resourceful debater was equally sought after in courts of law as in the council chamber or on the platform.

All over Gujarat and Kathiawar his services were in continual request. His impressive presence, polished manners and elegant attire—not to forget the velvet colour which adorned his coat—lent distinction to his personality, and marked him out from his contemporaries. Wherever he was wanted, he went with a travelling paraphernalia which was something to wonder at, and which often included a barber![10]

His extremely fastidious habits, which had to be scrupulously respected, added to the awe in which he was held by his clients and by the public generally. The combined battery of these forces bore down alike on the presiding judge and the opposing counsel and witnesses. Add to all these attributes of a skilful advocacy, and it is not surprising that his forensic triumphs were as great as any he achieved in the sphere of public life.

In 1887, we find Pherozeshah engaged in two cases which attracted considerable attention at the time. One was what was known as the Municipal Octroi case, in which a respected citizen of Broach, Edulji Muncherji, was charged with breach of trust. Messrs. Jardine and Pherozeshah defended the accused and after a lengthy hearing, secured his acquittal.

The verdict aroused considerable enthusiasm, and the more energetic among the good folks of Broach wanted to drag the carriage of the victorious counsel from the court to the bungalow where they were staying. The latter having declined the honour, their admirers had to content themselves with giving the heroes a hearty send-off.

Another matter in which Pherozeshah was engaged, and which added considerably to his reputation was the Cambay Inquiry which took place in the early part of 1887. In this trial, Wilson, the Collector of Kaira, stood charged with having made indecent overtures to a daughter of the Diwan of Cambay.

The high position of the parties and the nature of the offence invested the inquiry with a great deal of importance, and public interest was excited in an unusual degree. The Government of Lord

Reay, distinguished for the courage with which it dealt with moral lapses on the part of its servants, however, highly-placed or influential, appointed a commission of inquiry consisting of two responsible officials.

Mr. Inverarity, one of the greatest advocates who have ever practised in Indian courts, was engaged on behalf of the accused and Pherozeshah appeared for the complainant. The inquiry was held at Ahmedabad. In the absence of suitable accommodation, Pherozeshah and the attorney instructed him had to put up at the refreshment rooms at the railway station.

After a lengthy hearing, Wilson was found guilty of the charge laid against him, and this decision of the Commissioner was endorsed by the Government of Lord Reay after a careful consideration of the evidence in the case. Wilson appealed to the Secretary of State, tendering his resignation from service at the same time, and had the satisfaction of having his character duly white-washed.

Ever since the Ilbert Bill agitation had quickened political life in the country, the Bombay leaders, and particularly the brilliant triumvirate—Tyabji, Telang and Pherozeshah—were carrying on a ceaseless campaign for reforms in every branch of the administration. From various platforms and through diverse organizations, they laboured to promote the public good; but they were handicapped by the want of a newspaper which would support their policy, and inculcate from day to day the principles for which they stood. *The Times of India* was frankly anti-Indian in most of its views, and though the *Bombay Gazette* was sympathetic in its general attitude towards Indian aspirations it could not be regarded as expressing the popular point of view.[11]

Calcutta, Madras and even places of lesser importance boasted of one or two national organs, but the first city in India had apparently not the public spirit and enthusiasm to found and maintain an English daily conducted from the Indian stand point.

It was with a view to wiping out this reproach and supplying a real want that Pherozeshah in partnership with a well known journalist, Jehangir Murzban, undertook in 1888 to resuscitate the *Advocate of India*, which was languishing, at the time. It was then under the control of Dr. Blaney, an eminent citizen, whose manifold services to Bombay were afterwards rewarded by a grateful people with his statue erected in his lifetime.

The necessary arrangements were made and the proprietorship of the paper changed hands. In announcing that fact, the new management told the public what its policy was going to be in an article which is believed to have been written by Pherozeshah. After stating that those who had the direction of the paper in their hands had no intention of making rash promises of any sort, beyond that they would endeavour to discuss all public questions in a way which would promote the best interests of the country, the article went on to say:

> "There is, therefore, room in this Presidency for an English daily which would present Indian phenomena and facts, and approach and treat all Indian questions from an Indian point of view. We trust that this can be done with moderation as well as independence.
>
> "We hope to steer clear of two pitfalls, into one or other of which people in this country are apt to tumble in forming their judgements of men and events. We shall no more presume that all Englishmen, official or non-official, are malignant tyrants till they prove themselves the contrary, than we shall countenance the presumption that all natives, and especially educated natives are disloyal, seditious and generally ill-conditioned, till they establish their innocence. We steadily refuse to believe that Englishmen have a monopoly of one moiety of the sins in the decalogue, and the natives of this country of the other."[12]

In July 1889, Pherozeshah was elected Dean of the Faculty of Arts in the Bombay University. His rise to a position of influence in the University was somewhat rapid. Though his connection with it dated back to the year 1868, when he was appointed a Fellow on the recommendation of Sir Alexander Grant, for some years he did take very active interest in the deliberations of the Senate.

It was not till 1886, when he had attained eminence in other walks of life, that he began to play a leading part in the affairs of the University. About that time he joined in the discussion of various matters of importance. One of them related to the introduction of French as a second language in the curriculum of the University. Pherozeshah strongly supported the proposal, which had been moved by Justice Jardine and urged that the excellence of English literature was no reason why other modern languages should not be admitted. Students ought to be free to gather their knowledge from all sources. This view commended itself to a majority of the Senate, and the proposition was carried in spite of considerable opposition based on ancient prejudices.

Pherozeshah's interest in the cause of education was manifested in various other ways. He became one of the promoters of the Graduates' Association which was started in Bombay in April 1886. For the first few years, the Association showed considerable activity. It memorialized the University and the Government on all manner of educational questions, and did much useful work. Among other things, it obtained from the University the right of representation for graduates on the Senate. Pherozeshah's connection with it continued to the end. Two years after it was started he was appointed President, and enjoyed that position for a number of years.

In assessing Pherozeshah's public career, it is essential to remember that many of his principles were formed by his early training and environment. He had the good fortune to receive his education at the hands of a scholar of great attainments and singular breadth of view. When he went to England, it was with a mind fully equipped to receive the ideas and impressions which the West has to impart. While studying for the Bar, he came under the influence of Dadabhai Naoroji, who inspired him with his own burning love of the country and enthusiasm for the cause of progress and liberty. The young disciple was deeply interested in the world around him, and the social and political forces that were at work. He came under the principles remained unimpaired to the end, despite many disappointments. It was 'an agitated and expectant age,' as Gladstone called it, and its teachings deeply impressed themselves on his youthful mind.

Pherozeshah's temperament, equally with his early training,

was a great asset. He was a robust optimist, and he faced situations with serene courage and confidence. The hatred of enemies, the indifference of friends and the hostility of those in power and authority failed to shake his faith in the ultimate triumph of the cause he had espoused, and in the principles and methods by which he pursued it.

His literary tastes fostered this outlook on life. Dickens, Thackeray, Tennyson and the Bible were his favourites, and he carried these old friends with him wherever he went. In a conversation which he had shortly before his death with Chandavarkar, he said: "There is some solace in life, isn't there, when you call a small company of books like that your friends who have stood by you all through?" Referring to Tennyson, he went on to observe:

"Locksley Hall is my favourite: in Locksley Hall and Sixty Years After, you miss the fire and hopefulness and courage; it sounds like an old man's tale of murmur that the world has not behaved well with him.... I prefer the Tennyson of Locksley Hall, the poet of youth and middle age with a hopeful outlook on life, who saw the vision of the world and all the wonder that would be."[13]

It was this cheery optimism which sustained Pherozeshah through all difficulties and disappointments in his long and arduous career. It sustained him through the early struggles of the Congress, when he and his associates had to contend with hostility and ridicule on the one hand, and indifference and backsliding on the other. It sustained him through the dark and anxious days which followed the Partition of Bengal, when despair and despondency seized men's minds, and turned them aside from the paths of peaceful evolution. It sustained him through the grave crisis in national affairs precipitated by the *debacle* at Surat. Through all these difficult and often critical situations, while other men shrank back or wavered, he never lost heart, never felt shaken in his allegiance to the ideals and principles which he had made his own.

He was a firm believer, like many others of his generation, in the benefits of the British connection. No man more mercilessly exposed the defects, shortcomings and injustice which have often characterized the British administration of India, no man more courageously fought for the enlargement of the rights and liberties of the people. And yet, there was none who upheld the British connection more stoutly than he, recognizing as he did the weakness of his country's position and the essential justice and humanity, despite many lapses of English rule in India. Allied to this, was his deep-seated respect for constituted authority, which his early training had implanted in him. This was most strikingly exemplified in his civic career. While there was no critic of the administration more feared than he, the executive officers had no warmer supporter of their prestige and authority.

The distinguishing traits of Pherozeshah's methods of controversy were fearlessness, keen sense of fair play and regard for the decencies of public life. He hit out with refreshing vigour, but his denunciations were singularly free from mere aggressiveness or cheap rhetoric. His strength lay in the directness and uncompromising independence with which he expressed himself. From the days of Sir James Westland with his famous outburst about the introduction of the 'new spirit' officials in the Councils learnt to treat Pherozeshah with wholesome respect. Sometimes, however, they allowed their irritation to overcome them and lead them to personal attacks, as was done by Sir Fredrick Lely and Mr. Logan in the Bombay Council on occasions well remembered by all who witnessed the encounter. They never ventured to repeat the experiment, for the trouncing they got was not easily to be forgotten. And yet, in spite of the fact that Pherozeshah spent all his life in giving and receiving hard blows, he did not allow his sense of fair play to be blunted. He never hit below the belt. On the rare occasions on which he allowed himself to be carried away into making a hasty statement, he withdrew it as soon as his attention was drawn to its unfairness. He scrupulously observed the best traditions of public life, and was not wanting in generous appreciation of his opponents, whenever the occasion demanded it. The readiness with which he acknowledged their good intentions, and met all attempts at cooperation or conciliation, was in striking contrast to the general tendencies of the time.

The maturity of thought Pherozeshah showed at an early age was remarkable. The views which he expressed on educational problems as a young man were the views from which he found no occasion to differ throughout his career, and they invite comparison with his latest reflections on the subject. His thoughts on municipal reform when he was barely twenty-five betray the same maturity of mind, and might be said to be actually embodied in a municipal constitution which in its essentials has survived for fifty years. So also with his views on reforms in the Civil Service, and the benefits of India's participation in party politics. In all this, he was often in advance of his times, and in conflict with the opinions of men older and more experienced than himself.

The qualities which may be said to have contributed most to Pherozeshah's supremacy in public affairs were his intuitive judgement and his firm grasp of principles. His career provides many instances, for example his views on the Press Act and the South African problem are among the most recent of his political sagacity and the gift he had of seeing further than any of his contemporaries. It was largely owing to this that his colleagues often subordinated their views to his, even when they felt he was in the wrong. They invariably found that his judgement was sounder, his instinct surer.

For those who would lead their fellow-men through the dust and heat of political controversies, a certain gift of speech is more or less essential. Pherozeshah possessed it in ample measure. His oratory was characterized by considerable variety. The sonorous eloquence of his set speeches had a mid-Victorian flavour. It delighted the crowds who hung on his words on the Congress platform or in Town Hall. But his strength did not lie in that. There were other men, notably Surendranath Bannerji and Lal Mohun Ghosh, who excelled him in sheer eloquence. None, however, approached him, except at a respectful distance, in powers of debate, in the swift, decisive and masterly manner in which he floored an opponent. Quick to see the weak points of the case against him, he brought to bear on them all the resources of a capacious and well-trained intellect, and banter and ridicule generally finished what arguments left unaccomplished. Men felt themselves helpless as they listened to him and got convinced, sometimes against the evidence of their own senses. Thus it was he bore down all the opposition, whether on the floor of the University and the Corporation Hall, or in the Subjects Committee of the Congress, where he encountered some of the finest intellects in the country. People spoke of him as an autocrat. Perhaps he was, but when we see so many lesser men trying to lay down the law, we can appreciate the moderation with which, on the whole, Pherozeshah wielded the immense power which he enjoyed.[14]

An ardent lover of progress and liberty, Pherozeshah was strongly conservative in his outlook on some of the problems of the day. The love of ordered progress which his well-balanced mind and early training instilled into him, made him averse to all violent or sudden changes. Deeply imbued with the teachings of English history, he had a profound reverence for constitutional forms, and an abiding faith in the virtue of gradual and peaceful evolution of "freedom slowly broadening down from precedent to precedent." Always making the most of what he got, even if, as invariably happened, it fell short of what he had fought for, he set himself immediately to prepare for the next advance. He did not worry about the distant goal, but strove for what he thought the country was prepared for and had a right to demand, never doubting it would achieve its destiny in the process of time.

Pherozeshah was far and away the greatest political leader India had known. He never appealed to the masses as did Dadabhai Naoroji or Tilak, for instance. His hold was mainly over the educated and thinking section of the people. His impressive presence, personality and power of mind dominated all who worked with him or followed his lead. As was observed of Gladstone, "when he spoke, he uplifted debate from whatever rut of mediocrity it may have fallen into. That was the power of the orator. When he sat silent, his mere presence communicated to the House a sense of dignity and a moral strength easier to feel than to describe. That was the quality of the man." It was remarkable how the many gifted men with whom he was associated in various spheres of public life allowed their will and judgement to be subordinated to him. His personality dominated everybody and faithfully represented the feelings of even those who often differed from him, who found themselves helpless in his presence.

This supremacy becomes all the more remarkable over whom it was exercised. It is true that they were in no way inferior to Pherozeshah in vigour or intellect; there were others who closely rivalled him in gifts of speech and independence of character. There was none, however, who combined in him the qualities which compel the admiration and command the allegiance of one's fellow-men, and in that, apart from that undefinable something called personality, must be found an explanation of Pherozeshah's dominance over all who came in contact with him. There were men who made comparisons between him and Gokhale. Nothing could have been more foolish. The truth is that each did work complementary to that of the other, and what the other was probably not capable of accomplishing. Gokhale certainly could not have roused, as well as Pherozeshah did, the intelligentsia of the country from the apathy and even hostility with which a large section of it regarded the national movement. Gokhale could not have stood up as resolutely and as courageously as Pherozeshah did against injustice, oppression or autocracy. On the other hand, Pherozeshah was temperamentally incapable of the active and sustained educative work which Gokhale did from day to day, and the propaganda he carried on both in England and in India, and which owed its success as much to his high character as to his attainments. Comparisons between two such men are meaningless. Each was great in his own sphere, and together they made a notable contribution to the building up of the New India of which Dadabhai Naoroji had laid the foundations nearly fifty years ago.

The question has often been asked as to what would Pherozeshah have done had he been alive today? Over and over again in these five years have his speeches and writings been recalled by Extremists and Moderates alike, and curiously enough both sea of political opinion have claimed him as their own. In that, perhaps, one may find an explanation of his real position in politics. In his optimism, in his faith in the benefits of the British connection, and in his firm adherence to the methods of constitutional agitation, he belonged to the Moderates. In the vigour of his utterances, in the uncompromising independence of his attitude towards questions of principle, and in the tenacity and fearlessness with which he fought, he was a man after the heart of the Extremist. It is impossible to believe that with a leader of such eminence, the Moderate Party would have been what it is today, a sober and healthy element, no of education that has produced greatest men and given strength and reality to our demands, and which is calculated to divert the energies of the best of India's manhood from such forms of purposeful activities as have made for national progress.

What M.R. Jayakar said about the matter may well be quoted. After saying that Pherozeshah's life would long remain a landmark in India's political history, he went on to observe:

The few years which have elapsed since his death have seen a wonderful change come over this country. Perhaps, he would have been himself staggered, if he had lived to witness it. What his own attitude would have been now, it is difficult to say, as it is profitless to surmise. One can only say that with his characteristic freshness and vitality, he would perhaps have suited his leadership to the growing requirements of his countrymen, or else he would have stood aside from the mighty current, staggered at its volume, perhaps rejoicing at its depth, but unable to keep pace with its velocity.[15]

As Disraeli's biographer has remarked, "there is no need to labour further what is written broadly over the record which has been here presented." Sufficient has been said about the personality of Pherozeshah and his place in the national movement. Already other forces are at work, and other men have emerged. And may be that Pherozeshah's memory may become dimmed in the fast-changing political atmosphere of the country. But when the dust of controversy has settled, we may confidently leave to the judgement of history the achievements of the man and his impression upon the times in which he lived.[16]

REFERENCES

1. Mody, Homi, *Sir Pherozeshah Mehta, op. cit.*, p. 23.
2. Naoroji, Dadabhai, *Poverty and Un-British Rule in India, op. cit.*
3. *Ibid.*, p. 25.
4. Sastri, V. S. Srinivasa, *Life and Times of Sir Pherozeshah Mehta, op. cit.*, p. 46.
5. *Ibid.*, p. 47.
6. Naoroji, Dadabhai, *Poverty and Un-British Rule in India, op. cit.*, p. 47.
7. *Ibid.*

8. Mody, Homi, *Sir Pherozeshah Mehta, op. cit.*, pp. 30-31.
9. Lord Macaulay, *Minutes on Education.*
10. Mody, Homi, *Pherozeshah Mehta, op. cit.*, p. 60.
11. *Ibid.*
12. *Ibid.*, pp. 62-63.
13. Chintamani, C.Y., *Speeches and Writings of Sir Pherozeshah Mehta, op. cit.*, p. 87.
14. *Ibid.*
15. Jayakar, M.R., *The Story of My Life,* Vol. I (Bombay: Asia Publishing House), 1958.
16. *Ibid.*

3

LIBERAL NATIONALISM AND WORK IN IMPERIAL COUNCIL

Like T.H. Green and Dadabhai, Pherozeshah Mehta maintained that power should be rooted in the will, wishes, ideals, affection and aspirations of the people. Political strength is not substantiated by devising harsh measures, but receives solidity from calm discrimination, sagacity and sympathetic treatment. Political power has to be freed from the perversities of biases, unfounded and misleading prejudices and "the defects of their (executive officers) class and position."[1] It is a commonplace notion to base the roots of power in the cult of military force. From the sociological standpoint, power is founded upon community consensus and a response to the moral and social ideals of the people. No power structure can hope to perpetuate itself apart from a desire and a capacity to serve the common good. There was a school of politicians in England who maintained that India had been won by the sword and the Indian empire could be retained only by a policy of Machtpolitik. Refuting their position Mehta, pointed out:

"In preaching this gospel of might with regard to the government of this country, they have found a devoted supporter in England in Sir Fitz James. Stephen and a somewhat doubtful one in Lord Salisbury. They ridicule the policy of righteousness as one of weak sentiment and seem almost to adopt, with scarcely disguised approval, the vigorous summary of their position even recently by Bright in his own peculiarly hap manner, that having won India by breaking all the Ten Commandments, it is too late now to think of maintaining it on the principles of the Sermon on the Mount."[2]

But Pherozeshah refuted this interpretation of the modern history of India in terms of force. He believed that the foundations of British power in India were deeper. The preservation of power could not be separated from ethical consideration. He said:

"Englishmen don't do justice to themselves when they read India in this way though it cannot be denied that there are many pages in this history blotted by error and crime. England has won India not simply by the sword, but in a large measure by the exercise of high moral and intellectual qualities which have not only guided its victories, but have always been on the alert to neutralize its baneful influences."[3]

Pherozeshah analysed three baneful consequences of a policy of force applied by England in India. First, it would be creating great stains for England. She had to face the rivalaries and contests of France and Russia and in case of England being embroiled in any complications, India ruled by force would be a heavy burden on her. Secondly, despotism breeds its own Nemesis. English despot in India saturated with the sentiments of autocracy and having imbibed haughty sentiments and forceful predilections would prove a socially and politically damaging element in the English body politic. The attitudes of individual inflation and power intoxication generated in an atmosphere of social arrogance were bound to have repercussions even on British society after the return of the officers to the home country. Thirdly, a policy of force would involve the maintenance of a huge army which would mean the impoverishment and emasculation of the country. If the resources wasted in keeping a big army could be utilized in the material development of the country, that would be of immense benefit both to England and India.

Pherozeshah had faith in the values and the foundational principles of English culture and statesmanship. At the time of the election of Dadabhai Naoroji to the British House of Commons, he said:

"But it may be pardoned to us if, nurtured in some of the noblest traditions of English history we allow ourselves for a moment to be carried away by sentiment, if we venture to contemplate with some degree of emotion and reverence the spectacle of a native of India entering that very assembly in which, in terms of immoral eloquence,

Burke and Fox and Sheridan pleaded the cause of righteousness in the government of this country, where Macaulay saw in dim but prophetic vision the dawn of that day which may bring us our political enfranchisement, where Bright and Fawcett and Bradlaugh raised their voices of justice to millions of voiceless and alien people."[4]

He held that English statesmanship was illumined by a lofty conception of moral and political duty. Hence, he had faith that England would do justice to India. He had said in his presidential speech at the Calcutta-Congress of 1890:

"I have unbounded faith in the living and fertilizing principles of English culture and English civilization. It may be that, at times, the prospect may look dark and gloomy. Anglo-Indian opposition may look fierce and uncompromising. But my faith is large, even in Anglo-Indians…the higher and nobler nature which, in the end, must prevail and which has prevailed in so many honourable, distinguished and illustrious instances… When, in the inscrutable dispensation of Providence, India was assigned to the care of England, one can almost imagine that the choice was offered to her as to Israel of old: 'Behold I have placed before you a blessing and a curse; a blessing, if ye will obey the commandments of the Lord your God; a curse, if ye will not obey the commandments of the Lord your God but go after other Gods whom ye have not known.' All the great forces of English life and society, moral, social, intellectual, political, are if slowly, yet steadily and irresistibly, declaring themselves for the choice which will make the connection of England and India a blessing to themselves and to the whole world for countless generations. Our Congress...asks but to be allowed to join to the blessing which England will as surely earn as there is an 'Eternal that maketh for righteousness'."[5]

But although a believer in the permanence of the British empire, Pherozeshah Mehta would miss no opportunity to expose and ridicule the enterprise of conquest and commercial profits, which characterized Indians.

Pherozeshah was a keen patriot but he did not preach the concept of Indian freedom. He was anxious to maintain the character of the Indian National Congress. He was a person of clear thoughts but sober moderate political proposals who felt that the problems of politics could be solved not by alarm and excitement but by a loyal heart and unclouded reason. He believed in loyalty to the Crown and the permanence of the British Empire. He had trust in British righteousness and sympathy. As the chairman of the reception committee of the Indian National Congress session at Bombay, Pherozeshah firmly stated his faith and hope in the permanence of the British empire. He had an earnest solicitude for the safety and perpetuity of the empire of Great Britain because he was persuaded that there lay the roots of the welfare, happiness, prosperity and good government of the Indian people. He was sure that earnest and prayerful appeals of the Indian Intelligentsia would result in a reversal of retrograde measures and in the initiation of policies of wisdom and righteousness, and he hoped that the brilliant vision of Macaulay about Indians enjoying the felicities of glorious citizenship would be realised. These views may sound strange today in the environment of independent India but they should be isolated from the context of the situation when they were pronounced. It was not his fault but it was the limitation of the situation. In those days the powerful engine of British imperialism was firmly planted in the country and it would have been too risky to sponsor the concept of freedom.

The moderate leaders of India were opposed to centralization and pleaded for increasing local autonomy. Ranade, Pherozeshah and Surendranath advocated extension of the power of local authorities. Pherozeshah had keen interest in the advancement of local self-government. He was in favour of local Independence to municipal bodies but he never stood for independence without control. On the question of control over local authorities, he referred to the view of John Stuart Mill and Herbert Spencer. He said: "We know that the highest authorities on the subject—Herbert Spencer and John Stuart Mill—have pointed out that you must have external or internal check on the working of these municipal bodies, you must not have both."[6] He wanted the fullest control over local authorities but he also urged that something should be left to the local authorities so that they would feel that control was emanating from them and not from outside. He would not plead for independence free from all control but the local bodies had to be given some real power and responsibility. The sense of utter impotency which the elected members felt in the local bodies of Indian cities was responsible for the unsatisfactory character of municipal administration. Hence a genuine participant local government was desirable. Pherozeshah also quoted John Stuart Mill and Herbert Spencer on the problem vesting executive functions in a single officer and not in a board or sub-committees.

The extension of educational opportunities was one of the cardinal tenets in the political philosophy of the Indian Moderates. Education, they regarded as the key to creative life. They held that the emancipation of mind was one of the priceless possessions of the citizen. Pherozeshah was in favour of extension of public education. Being a liberal he had faith in rationalism and enlightenment.

He pleaded for both intellectual and moral education. History and humanities, according to him, were the schools of morality. He said:

"There is no doubt that an intelligent and educated population is the best means of developing indefinitely the resources of a country. On the continent this idea has of late gained immense ground. It was first started by those grand statesmen of French Revolution, even as they were hurling defiance and armies at a coalition of almost all the crowded heads of Europe. And though the original plans of Condorect and Robespierre fell through the time, yet ever since France, Germany, Italy and Switzerland have been sparing no efforts, even in times of trouble and difficulty, to reconstruct their systems of public education under the direct administration, management and support of the State."[7]

Education alone could permeate Indians with a higher ideal of public and private obligation and loyalty. Mehta, however, drew his intellectual roots only from western culture. He had no acquaintance with Sanskrit and, hence, in his paper entitled "Educational System of Bombay", he denounced "Sanskrit language and literature as 'useless and even mischievous', as far as they went, for the purposes of a regeneration at all commensurate with a nineteenth century civilization."

These ideas evolved during his work in the Imperial Council.

With the creation of the enlarged Councils under the Act of 1891, Pherozeshah emerged into a larger arena. His activities in the Congress, the University and the Corporation had given him already a commanding position among the public men of India. But it was not until he found admission into the Supreme Legislative Council that his brilliant intellect and remarkable powers of debate obtained their proper field of exercise, and disclosed to the public the full force of his personality.

The election took place in October 1893. According to the rules framed under the Indian Councils Act, the non-official members of the Provincial Legislative Council had the right of sending one representative to the Viceregal Council, and their choice unanimously fell on Pherozeshah.

Recognition of a different kind came to Pherozeshah shortly afterwards and a short digression must be made in order to notice it. The New Year's Honours List of 1894 contained the announcement of the conferment on him of the C.I.E. The distinction was very modest indeed but such as it was, it gave general satisfaction, and there was a chorus of congratulations from all quarters.

The esteem in which Pherozeshah was widely held at this stage of his career was greatly increased by the splendid work he did in the Supreme Council. On the numerous questions that came up before that body, he spoke with an ability, fearlessness and mastery of argument which delighted his many admirers all over the country. He introduced indeed a new spirit into the Council, and while the country applauded, officialdom was furious at the change of tone and temper in the opposition which he had brought about.

The first measure of importance, in the discussion of which Pherozeshah made himself felt, was the Cotton Duties Bill, which came up for consideration in the Imperial Council in December 1894. With the advent of Lord Ripon, a robust Free trader, and aided by the prosperous condition of the finances of 1882, all import duties were abolished, except on salt and liquor, by the then Finance Minister, Sir Evelyn Baring.

Financial exigencies, however, rendered necessary in 1894 the practical restoration of the tariff of 1875, under which everything had to be imported at a five per cent duty. That the Lancashire interest might not suffer thereby, Sir Henry Fowler, who was then the presiding deity at Whitehall, imposed an excise duty of five per cent on all cotton yarns below 30s, to which the Government of India had to yield, eliciting from *The Times of India* the remark that the forces of China had not surrendered more helplessly before their pursuing enemies than Lord Elgin's Government had done before a masterful Secretary of State.

When the report of the Select Committee on the Cotton Duties Bill was presented in the Supreme Council, Fazulbhoy Visram, a well-known figure in the commercial world of Bombay, moved an amendment with a view to remedying injustice. In supporting the amendment, Pherozeshah strongly attacked the principle underlying the Bill.

"That principle and that policy are that the infant industries of India should be strangled in their birth if there is the remotest suspicion of their competing with English manufactures protest against such a policy not only in its present immediate operation, but as establishing a most pernicious precedent."[8]

Ultimately, the amendment was defeated by eleven votes to nine, and "for the first time in the history of British rule in India, a measure was placed upon the statute book which no one has ever dreamed of defending as being promoted in the interests of the country affected by it.

Another Bill which provoked a lively debate was that dealing with an amendment of the Cantonments Act of 1889. The manner in which it was introduced in the Imperial Council raised in an acute form the question of the constitutional relations between the "Great Moghul" at Simla and the less imposing but more irresponsible autocrat at Whitehall. The Legal Member in charge of it had admitted at the time of its introduction that it was a Bill which had been brought forward "by direction of Her Majesty's Government with the object of complying, if the Legislative Council should think fit to do so, with the requirements of the majority of the Commission which sat on the question of the examination in cantonments."[9]

When the Bill came up for second reading, Sir Griffith Evans criticized the manner of its introduction, and dealt at some length with the position of the Council in relation to the Secretary of State for India. He protested against the latter's assumption of a legislative initiative which he did not think the constitution of the Indian Government intended he should assume. The Secretary of State had done so by virtue of his supreme executive control, but it was unconstitutional and in the nature of an usurpation, and if it was persisted in, it would lead to the straining of the whole machinery of the Government of India.

Such spirited criticisms of the action of Whitehall undoubtedly lifted the debate from the region of the common-place. But the point of view of Evans and another eminent representative of Bengal, though argued with considerable skill, was not quite correct. It was left to Pherozeshah to distinguish clearly between the vast and almost autocratic powers of the Viceroy in certain spheres with his subordination to the Secretary of State in others. He started by enunciating a principle which admitted of no dispute, viz., that the Government of the country was really in the hands of the House of Commons, which exercised its authority through ministers who possessed its confidence.

The Secretary of State had the authority of the House to sustain him, and the responsibility to carry out its at his behest with all lawful means open to him. August as the office of the Viceroy was, it could not be said that it was independent of Parliament. This subordination was perfectly consistent with the possession of a large and preponderating measure of influence, which the opinions and recommendations of so highly placed an individual could not fail to command in the final decision of Indian questions.

Pherozeshah, for once, accepted this constitutional position without any regret. He did not believe in the theory of "the man on the spot", and he regarded the ultimate control of the House of Commons, exercised through the Secretary of State, as a more or less wholesome influence on Indian polity.

After his discourse on the constitutional aspect of the measure before the Council, Pherozeshah went on to deal with the genesis of the Bill, and showed that it was merely designed to give statutory form to that which was already the subject of rules and regulations, which in practice had given rise to various abuses.

At this point, he laid his finger on a grave defect of Indian legislation, viz., the practice of reserving to executive authorities the power of making rules and regulations to provide for matters, which ought to be included in the Acts themselves. Under such a system, according to him, assurance and undertakings were made to take the place of definite provisions, which were either forgotten, or what was more dangerous, interpreted in all sorts of wonderful ways.

The history of Indian legislation provides abundant instances—not the least notable being the Morley-Minto Reform scheme of Acts charged with liberal intentions being shorn of all their progressive character by the reservation to Government of an indefinite power of making rules and regulations.

The Bill was referred to a Select Committee, and having been modified to meet the objections raised against it, it was passed unanimously at the February sitting of the Council.

The activities of the legislative machine did not end here. It had several more gills to grind out. We shall notice only one of them, which was the subject of severe criticism in the Council and outside, and which gave rise to an explosion of temper on the part of the Finance Member, which rendered Pherozeshah famous through the length and breadth of the land. This was a Bill for the amendment of the Police Act of 1861. Under the Act, the Local Government was empowered to quarter a punitive police force in any district which was found to be in a disturbed or dangerous state, and to recover the cost from the inhabitants thereof generally.

The amending Bill sought to enable the authorities to recover the cost in certain cases from the turbulent section only and not necessarily from all the inhabitants. It also sought to make it possible to levy contributions from absentee owners of property, when their action caused or contributed to the disturbed state of the locality. There were two other important alterations proposed, namely, the power to levy compensation for injury caused by the misconduct of any party, and to regulate processions which were likely to lead to breach of the public peace.

Under cloak of redressing a wrong, the Bill was in fact an

attempt to invest magistrates with extraordinary powers in supersession of the ordinary courts of law. They were to have a free hand in singling out individuals for punishment. The guilty and the innocent were equally at the mercy of the executive. Those who lived in the disturbed area were just as much liable to punishment as absentee landlords who might be hundreds of miles away.

The measure was in fact nothing else but an attempt, as Pherozeshah characterized it, to convict and punish individuals without a judicial trial, under cover of executive measures for the preservation of order. This was an opinion which was not confined to noisy agitators, but, unfortunately for Government, was shared by some of its own officers. The language employed by Pherozeshah, which raised a breeze in the Council Hall, creating an atmospheric disturbance which was felt far and wide, was, therefore, none too strong:

"My Lord, I cannot conceive of legislation more empirical, more retrograde, more open to abuse, or more demoralizing. It is impossible not to see that it is a piece of that empirical legislation so dear to the heart of executive officers, which will not and cannot recognize the scientific fact that the punishment and suppression of crime, without injuring or oppressing innocence, must be controlled by judicial procedure, and cannot be safely left to be adjudged upon the opinion and moral certainties of men believing themselves to be capable, honest and conscientious...

"Empirical and retrograde, as it is, this new proposed legislation would be no less demoralizing to the executive officers concerned. I have not the least desire to speak disparagingly of executive officers, most of whom, I have no doubt, are anxious to perform their duties conscientiously and to the best of their ability. But it would be idle to believe that they can be free from the biases, prejudices and defects of their class and position."[10]

Sir James Westland, the Finance Member, was furious at the thought that anyone should venture to speak so irreverently as Pherozeshah had done to the idols of the official hierarchy. Sacrilegious hands had been laid on their fair name and reputation, and the members felt horrified at the idea. His petulant outburst, the echoes of which were heard for a long time, may well be quoted in full:

"As the first member of Your Excellency's Executive Council who has an opportunity of speaking after extraordinary observations which have fallen from the Honourable Mr. Mehta, I desire to enter a protest against the new spirit which he has introduced into this Council. I have never heard the conduct of the administrative officers of the Government, as a whole, mentioned here without admiration of the qualities they bring to the execution of their duty, and their anxious endeavour to do their work with even-handed justice.

"Today for the first time within the walls which have been distinguished by the presence, through half a century and more of the most eminent of the executive officers of Government, who have contributed to the framing and the consolidation of the Indian Empire, I hear them all arraigned as a class as biased, prejudiced, utterly incapable of doing the commonest justice, and unworthy of being relied on to do the duties which this legislature imposes upon them.

"From Your Excellency downwards, every executive officer falls under the ban of the Honourable Member's denunciations, and I for one protest against any Honourable Member so far forgetting the responsibility he owes to his position as to take advantage of it to impugn, by one general all comprehensive accusation, not only the capacity but even the honesty and fairness of the members of a most distinguished Service—a Service of which it is my pride to have been a member."[11]

This extraordinary outburst was quite uncalled for, and Pherozeshah immediately repudiated any intention of indulging in such general charges or imputations as the Finance Member had read into observations. The incident set the country attaining for weeks together. Sir James Westland's petulant criticisms had the effect, unexpected by their author, of bringing about a keener appreciation of the great work done by the Bombay member in the reformed Council.

It was felt that a "new spirit" had indeed been at work. The frank, free and fearless criticisms of Pherozeshah were felt to mark the beginnings of a new era in politics. It was a novel experience to find the acts and policies of the Government held up in their very presence to a merciless examination both as regards their intention and their methods. It was considered as something good, a modest measure of reform which had converted the Legislative Councils from being mere machines for the registration of official decrees and fiats into assemblies where the people's voice could be heard, led and a little daylight let into the mysterious processes which surrounded Government measures.

It was the recognition of the elective principle in the creation of the Councils, for which educated public opinion had fought so strenuously, that had made this possible. *The Tribune* of Lahore in its issue of January 30, 1895, put the issue very clearly while commenting on the work accomplished by Pherozeshah:

"There is one voice in the Imperial Legislative Council which has struck a note not yet heard inside the walls of the Council chamber. When the Hon. Mr. P. M. Mehta. scornfully spoke of the exchange compensation during the debate on the Tariff Bill, the members of the Executive Council and very high officials winced for the first time.

"What they had been accustomed to read in newspapers, and to find in reports of public meetings, which they never attended, had at length broken through the inviolability of the Council hall, and the strong clear voice of fearless criticism rang upon their ears for the first time. For the first time also, the public saw what stuff some of the highest officials are made of.

"Sir James Westland unconsciously uttered a great truth when he spoke of the new spirit introduced by Mr. Mehta into the Council. Yes, there is a new spirit, not introduced by Mehta, but which has first found utterance through him. The new spirit was introduced by the Act of 1882."[12]

It would be tedious to dwell over the passage of the Police Bill into law. It emerged from the Select Committee modified in a few particulars, but retaining most of its objectionable features. As Pherozeshah observed, some paint and some powder had no doubt been used to soften the features, and new and flowing habiliments had been thrown over the gaunt spectre. But for all that, it remained essentially a measure designed to give District Magistrates, ostensibly for the purpose of prevention of crime and for the preservation of law and order, wide and autocratic powers, which would in practice be exercised by the police on whom the magistrates had by force of circumstances to lean very largely.

The Bill, in its final stages, had a somewhat rough passage. The thin lines of the Opposition, led by Pherozeshah, advanced again and again towards attack, but they left no impression on the solid phalanx that was arrayed against them. As Pherozeshah observed with a touch of biting sarcasm, on whichever side might be the arguments, the votes were certainly on the side of the Honourable Member who was in charge of the Bill. Amendments after amendments pressed by Pherozeshah, Babu Mohini Mohan Roy, the Maharaja of Durbhanga and Gangadhar Rao Chitnavis, the doyen of the Council, were thrown out, and the Bill, passed into law substantially as it stood, and fresh weapons were added to the armoury of a police notorious for its corruption.

In the record of Pherozeshah's activities in the Council at this period, a brief reference must be made to the role he played as the spokesman of enlightened Hindu opinion on the question of the restitution of conjugal rights. The English ecclesiastical law provided for imprisonment as a method of compelling a refractory wife to obey a decree for restitution.

Before 1887, it was very doubtful whether such a law could apply to India. In that year, the Law Member, Whitley Strokes, the author of the famous work on the Anglo-Indian Codes, seized with a desire for uniformity, introduced the clause for imprisonment in the Civil Procedure Code, which was then being amended. A large proportion of the lower classes in India found the change very welcome, and made considerable use of the procedure sanctioned by the law. This went on for some years until the famous Rukhmabai case brought out, in an aggravated form, the hardship inflicted in individual cases by the enforcement of the provision for imprisonment.

There was considerable agitation over the matter, and Government decided to take the first opportunity of amending the law so as to make imprisonment discretionary. Accordingly, when the amendment of the Civil Procedure Code was taken in hand in

1894, a clause was inserted in the Bill to that effect. In the Select Committee, however, orthodox Hindu opinion triumphed and the clause was deleted.

When the Bill came up for discussion on February 28, 1895, Pherozeshah moved for the re-insertion of the clause in a modified form, whereby the Courts were empowered to order in fit cases that a decree for restitution should not be enforced by imprisonment. He disclaimed all desire to meddle with so peculiar and complex a system of social life and religion as Hinduism, as he held that whatever reforms might be desirable and necessary should be left to be developed by the action of time and education. What he sought to do was to remove an excrescence which had been engrafted upon Hinduism by an extraneous jurisprudence; and he maintained he was representing the best Hindu opinion on the matter, the opinion which might, for instance, have been put forward by men like the late Telang. He did not agree with those who believed that "the distinguishing features of the Hindu social system as regards the relations of the sexes were distrust and depression of women."[13]

The Council, however, was influenced by the strength of conservative feeling manifested in and out of it against the change, and though Sir Alexander Miller and some other official members appeared to be in sympathy with the spirit of the amendment, the only member to support it, besides the mover, was Chitnavis, and Pherozeshah found that he was really not voicing, as he claimed, the conservative and orthodox view of the matter.

This record of work, accomplished during a strenuous and memorable session, may fittingly be brought to a close with a reference to the Budget debate. Under the Indian Councils Act of 1892, the submission of the financial statement to the Council provided practically the only opportunity of criticizing the administration and influencing its policy.

It became an annual feast at which oratorical fireworks were let off with reckless prodigality, and like all fireworks made a momentary impression and left no traces behind. The whole thing was more or less a solemn farce, and not a little tiresome. The official members regarded the long orations as the vapourings of amateurs not to be considered very seriously, and listened with as much patience as a bureaucracy, supremely conscious of its own wisdom, can command.

It was rarely that a Pherozeshah or a Gokhale appeared on the scene and made officialdom wince under the lash of their able and incisive criticisms. Their Budget speeches were something different from mere rhetorical exercises, and though the replies of official members were accustomed to strike a note of lofty superiority, it is not too much to say the Treasury benches were never very happy during the ordeal.

On the present occasion, Pherozeshah directed his chief attack against the alarming growth of expenditure in India. He supported it by quoting the views of past Finance Members, Sir Auckland Colvin, Sir David Barbour and others. They had practically admitted that the constitution of the Government of India was such that there was no efficient control over expenditure, and that every member of the council, except the Finance Minister, was not only not responsible for financial equilibrium, but was directly interested in spending money.

The enormous growth of expenditure had also been pointed out in an able representation submitted in March 1894, by the Bombay Presidency Association, of which Pherozeshah was then President. In dealing with that representation, the latter observed, the Finance Member had grown very facetious over the pretensions of native amateurs to show the most distinguished service in the world how they ought to govern India, and his mirth had been specially aroused at their pretensions to teach him how to manage Indian finance; but he would not be able to say of the views of his predecessors in office that they were the views of clumsy and pretentious politicians, though they had confirmed in the most remarkable manner the contentions advanced by the Association. And the fact that stood out prominently from this testimony, expert or otherwise, was that military expenditure was growing at an alarming rate, absorbing fully one half of the whole net revenue of the Government of India. If it was not possible to reduce it by any curtailment in the strength of the army, or any halt in the forward policy, then there was no other remedy for the embarrassment of Indian finance than to urge England and the English Treasury to be just and equitable in their demands for the cost and equipment of the British troops they supplied, which was what the Government of India themselves had urged in a dispatch dated February 8, 1879.

In sharp and striking contrast to this alarming growth of expenditure, Pherozeshah went on, the amount spent on education was just two per cent of the net revenue, which was about equal to the sum swallowed by the Exchange Compensation Allowance.

Sir James might wax sarcastic over "the united wisdom of the native gentlemen interested in politics who met at Christmas at Lahore to show us how we ought to govern India," but the facts and figures which the speaker had adduced spoke for themselves, and they justified his argument that the Financial Statement could not be regarded as satisfactory, and that the Budget was not based on principles of sound finance.

It was in the fitness of things that the splendid work done in the Council by Pherozeshah should receive recognition at the hands of his countrymen. The public appreciated, as it had never done before, what manner of man he was. He was no demagogue delighting the crowd by violence of language or ideas, nor a rhetorician losing himself in mere words, nor too a professional politician seeking his own advancement. He had the keen eye of a great general who makes the most effective disposition of the forces under his command, and is quick to seize every tactical advantage. He was formidable in attack, and very clever at effecting a retreat from a position which was found to be untenable. Those who crossed swords with him had thus a wholesome respect for him. These outstanding traits, in which he stood unrivalled had found their full scope on the floor of the Legislative Council, and his achievements there had evoked an admiration and enthusiasm which were remarkable.

Even that great organ of reactionary opinion, *The Pioneer*, could not withhold a tribute, and in an appreciation of his life and career—enlivened by personal touches about his handsome appearance, his splendid residence and the variety and costliness of his furniture—spoke of him as one of the ablest and most eminent leaders of Western India, and next to Dadabhai Naoroji, the most intellectual man among his set.

The first of the many functions held in Pherozeshah's honour took the shape of an evening party given by his old friend W.C. Bonnerji at his house in Park Street. A few days afterwards, a dinner was held in the Town Hall, at which Man Mohan Ghosh, another fellow-student at Lincoln's Inn, presided. A much bigger function was held in the same place shortly afterwards, when the citizens of Calcutta gave a public entertainment to mark their appreciation of the services of their distinguished countryman from Bombay.

The series of entertainments constituted a demonstration which was not without political significance. Seldom had Calcutta witnessed such large and representative gathering. In honouring him, Bengal showed that the national spirit was truly at work, bringing about a community of thought and feeling and breaking down the barriers of race and religion. Later, when Pherozeshah was in the midst of his own choice circle of friends at the Ripon Club banquet, he acknowledged with much warmth the hospitality which the people of Calcutta had shown him, and which had made him feel more keenly than ever that he was an Indian of Indians.

On April 1, 1879 Pherozeshah returned to Bombay, loaded with honours, and was welcomed at the Byculla station by a large number of friends and admirers. The city had decided to give him a hearty reception and had arranged various entertainments in his honour. Public enthusiasm was intense, and there was a general desire to commemorate his services in a tangible form. Some suggested the erection of a statue; others wanted a more ambitious and useful memorial. All classes of people vied with each other to do honour to one who had come to be regarded as "the uncrowned King of Bombay."

Shortly after his arrival, Pherozeshah was re-elected to the provincial Council by the Corporation. In view of the fact that his duties as a member of the Supreme Council sometimes took him away from Bombay, there was some talk of bringing forward a new candidate, but there being a strong feeling that he was indispensable, he consented to be proposed for re-election, and was unanimously returned as the representative of the Corporation. It was in the natural course of things, for, as a writer observed, his influence in civic affairs was so predominant that the records of the Corporation for some years might be searched almost, if not quite in vain, for an instance in which any proposition or amendment he had brought forward had not been carried. On one occasion, when the question of the Police charges was under consideration, the Corporation had actually postponed a decision as Pherozeshah happened to be away.

The Ripon Club was appropriately enough the first in Bombay to offer its homage. The head of the Parsi community, the third Sir Jamsetjee Jejeebhoy, presided over a large and distinguished company, and paid a handsome tribute to "the force of character, the steady aim, the zeal, industry and fearless eloquence" with which the Bombay Member of the Supreme Legislative Council had always carried on the fight for liberty and progress.

The next scene of triumph was laid in the Novelty Theatre, a hideous structure of corrugated iron sheets, which did duty in the old days as the premier play-house of Bombay. There, on April 20, 1879 a large and enthusiastic gathering, convened under the auspices of the Bombay Presidency Association, testified to the influence and popularity of one who was by common consent the greatest citizen of Bombay.

The Eighth Provincial Conference, held at Belgaum on May 4, 1895, was the next to place on record its appreciation. Pherozeshah attended the Conference and was given a hearty reception at the station as his special saloon steamed in. For weeks Belgaum had been preparing to give a rousing welcome to the man on whom the eyes of all India were centred for the time being. All interest in the proceedings gathered round his personality, and it was a great disappointment to the people when it was known later that indisposition would deprive them of the opportunity of hearing him.

The resolution recording Pherozeshah's "masterly services" was moved by Gokhale, then unknown to fame, but recognized by those who knew him as a young man of brilliant promise. He quoted a comparison made by a shrewd observer of men and things of the three greatest personalities in the public life of Western India.

That critic had said that Telang was always lucid and cultured, Mehta vigorous and brilliant and Ranade profound and original.

Gokhale said he agreed, with the verdict, but did not think it contained the whole truth. Though some people thought that Mehta's particular gift were vigour of intellect and brilliancy, it did not follow he was in anyway deficient in the other qualities. He was to a great extent a happy combination of the independence and strength of character of Mandlik, the lucidity and culture of Telang and the originality and wide grasp of Mr. Ranade. This was praise indeed!

It was not until the end of 1895 that the various addresses, voted to Pherozeshah, were presented to him at a public meeting held in the Gaiety Theatre on December 20. It was a remarkable demonstration. Long before the appointed hour, large numbers of people flocked to the theatre; the late arrivals could not even find space to stand. Every inch of ground was occupied and the theatre was filled to suffocation. A large crowed collected outside, and gave a rousing welcome to Pherozeshah who on entering the hall, was given another ovation.

Rahimtulla Sayani, who was in the chair, called upon Chandavarkar to read the address of the citizens of Bombay. The address voted at the Eighth Provincial Conference was next read by its chairman, Wacha. With a neat little speech, Sayani presented the two addresses enclosed in beautiful silver caskets.

As Pherozeshah rose to reply and looked upon the vast gathering, representative of every community and section, he might well have felt it was a moment to be proud of. Year after year he had risen steadily in the public estimation, and now, while still in the prime of life, he stood before his countrymen with a career and reputation second to none in the whole land. He rose to the occasion, and delivered a speech which was rated among his greatest efforts. It was mostly confined to a slashing reply to the calumnies and misrepresentations of the Indian point of view with which the enemies of Indian aspirations sought to scotch all attempts at progress and reform. It was at once a vindication of the claims of the educated classes to voice the national aspirations, and a condemnation of the superior critics who were never tired of deriding the aims and methods of the Congress and its leaders.

It was a great speech and swept the vast audience off its feet. Its conclusion was greeted with applause which continued for some minutes.

From amongst a mass of remarkable tributes, Sir William Wedderburn's review of Pherozeshah's career in the columns of *India* arrests particular attention. So also does an observation of *The Indian Spectator*, which wrote approvingly of a suggestion which was on everybody's lips:

"Bombay, we see, has at last fired off her double-barrelled gun at Mr. Mehta's devoted head. And great has been the noise thereof. But is Bombay going to sleep after this explosion? If there is anything in it, she ought to send Mr. Mehta to the House of Commons. That would be the best reward of his labours, and the most profitable investment that Bombay could make of its spare cash.

"We have always felt the need of a speaker and debater of Mr. Mehta's eminence at St. Stephen's, and should be rejoiced to see a practical turn given to the appreciation undoubtedly cherished for him by all classes of the community. A little timely organization would lead to the attainment of this truly national object."[14]

It would be difficult to speculate about Pherozeshah's political career had he entered Parliament, as so many of his friends and followers wished him to do. There was no room, of course, in that most critical assembly in the world, for the mid-Victorian style of oratory which he sometimes affected, but his unrivalled powers of debate and readiness of speech and argument would certainly have compelled attention.

Gifts such as his would have made their mark anywhere, and it was a thousand pities the Mother of Parliaments never knew the greatest political leader and debater that modern India had produced.

The strain of work in so many fields told on Pherozeshah at this period, and he kept indifferent health. The robustness of his constitution and the regularity of his habits had enabled him so far to withstand the wear and tear of an exceedingly active political career.

His mode of life, careful at all times, tended to becomes more and more rigid as time went on. In early years, he was fond of club life, and belonged to the small circle which constituted the somewhat exclusive Excelsior Club. He got tired of it after a time, and decided on starting an institution modelled on up-to-date lines, and with a constitution different from that of other institutions in that it was not to be merely a coterie of friends, but was to be open to every person of respectability in society. The Ripon Club thus came to be founded in 1885, and at once attracted towards it a large number of men of light and leading in the community.

There, for some years, Pherozeshah spent his evenings, often dining with a few friends and spending a couple of hours in the boisterous game of *chaupat*, the favourite amusement of the high and low in those days. After a time, he dropped out, and the Club saw less and less of him, until the 'Friends in Council' dinners were instituted by his close companion, C. M. Cursetjee, at which members of other communities were often invited and which came to be looked upon as more or less political gatherings. Pherozeshah enjoyed these functions, to which his presence attracted very interesting company.

Towards middle life, however, his habits became sedentary and monotonous and came to be governed by a sort of timetable. He seldom dined out or entertained, or was seen at public gatherings. At the same time, the attention he bestowed on his person and the care he devoted to his health became more and more exacting. To such habits of life may be attributed the good health and mental vigour which he enjoyed so long. Few constitutions, however well perserved, can prove equal, however to a heavy and continued strain in a tropical climate, and Pherozeshah showed signs of breakdown on his return from Calcutta.

One of the first things he did was to sever his connection with the Imperial Legislative Council, to which he had been reelected only a couple of months before. On January 26, 1896, he wired his resignation to the Viceroy. Finding himself unable to take any part in the deliberations of the Council, he felt there was no other course open to him but to make room for someone who could actively represent the Presidency, particularly as the Cotton Duties Bill, in which the commercial world of Bombay was keenly interested, and other measures of importance were coming up for discussion.

The resignation caused widespread regret. It was generally felt that the Imperial Council was much the poorer for the loss of a member whose activities had evoked universal admiration. The Indian Press with one voice deplored the circumstance which had compelled his resignation at a moment when his presence was sorely needed.

Though ill-health compelled Pherozeshah to curtail some of his activities, he controlled the currents of public life as well as before, and so far as Bombay was concerned, there was hardly a movement which did not depend upon his guidance or direction. There were other leaders of undoubted ability and influence, but whenever any difficulty arose, they instinctively felt that his presence and counsel were necessary. The direct and active influence he exercised over public affairs was thus as great, even when directed from the hill-top of Matheran, as when he thundered in the growing unrest in the country.

The University claimed a considerable share of Pherozeshah's attention in spite of ill-health. He took up a fighting attitude on the question of examination reforms and strongly criticised the Syndicate for declining to embody the recommendations made in that behalf by a committee, and for trying to defy the authority of the Senate. He lent his support to Ranade in the strenuous endeavours made by that eminent scholar and educationist to afford some relief to the harassed student from the crushing burden of examinations. Though rarely coming in contact with the student world, he had a sympathetic understanding of its wants and difficulties; his outlook was not that of a pedagogue or a drill-sergeant.

The attitude of the Government towards the University provided another topic for discussion. It was in the time of Lord Dufferin that the first steps were taken towards the inauguration of a policy of veiled hostility to the cause of higher education, which was regarded as the root cause of the Senate, the Corporation or the Council.

Confidential and semi-confidential circulars were issued to local authorities to curtail the grants to universities and colleges, and gradually to withdraw the State subsidy altogether. This policy had resulted in the steady reduction of the grant to the Bombay University, which had come down from Rs. 20,000 to Rs. 5,000, and against which the Senate at the instance of Pherozeshah had entered an emphatic protest. The latter had carried the fight into the Council also, and held up the Government to scorn for the niggardly treatment meted out to the University. But these protests had proved unavailing, and the University had now been informed that it could safely be left independent of financial support from provincial revenues, and that no provision had accordingly been made for a grant in the Budget of 1896-97.

On July 27, 1896, the Senate, at the instance of Pherozeshah, supported by Ranade, decided to make a representation to Government urging them to reconsider their decision to withdraw the annual grant. He contended that although the University had established a financial equilibrium, it was still not in a position to carry out certain essential reforms and that in any case the contribution should not have been stopped without giving the University an opportunity to state its case.[15]

He said he knew that the Government had already made up its mind, but the education he had received had taught him that the success of an Englishman lay in the fact that he never knew when he was defeated, and he wished the Senate would not acknowledge defeat likewise. It was a more or less hopeless position, but he hoped the majority of the fellows would regard the meeting not as one of condolence, but rather as one of doctors in consultation over a patient who was in extremes, but not quite dead as yet!

When the Legislative Council met at Poona on August 17, 1896, Pherozeshah attacked with much vigour the policy responsible for the cutting down of the Government dole.

It was in the nineties that the subject of the treatment of Indian settlers in South Africa began to engage the attention of their countrymen in India and the outside world. Beginning with a few occasional acts of hostility, the South African States, British and Boer, soon began to vie with each other in the severity of the disabilities they sought to impose upon the Indian immigrant population, whose nationality they despised, but whose labour they valued. It would be a painful and profitless task to detail the various indignities which were heaped from time to time upon a class of industrious and law-abiding people whose only sin was that they were frugal in their habits. The story of their wrongs forms one of the blackest pages in the history of British Imperialism.

The Indian community in South Africa, alarmed at the growing hostility manifested towards it on all sides, organized itself for defence under the leadership of one of the most extraordinary figures that have ever trod the public stage in this or any other country. M.K. Gandhi, for it was none other than he, deeply moved by the wrongs done to his countrymen, threw away a lucrative practice at the Bar, and consecrated himself to the task of securing for them their just rights as citizens of the British Empire. He was subjected to hardships and indignities which would have broken most men. But he was of the stuff of which the truly great are made. On one occasion in the main street of Durban, he was kicked, whipped, and stale fish and other things were thrown at him which hurt his eye and cut his ear, and his hat was taken off his head. Through the help of the police he was escorted to the house of an Indian, and when a threatening crowd blockaded the house, he had to be taken away to the police station, disguised as a constable.

He continued to fight with courage and determination. He memorialised the Colonial Office and the Indian Government from time to time, pointing out the iniquity of the legislative measures which their weakness and indifference had enabled the South African States to impose upon the helpless Indians. He carried on active propaganda work, and appealed to his countrymen in India for their sympathy and support.[16] In August 1895, we find him writing to Pherozeshah from Durban on behalf of the Indian community, appealing for the latter's help in connection with the Immigration Law Amendment Act passed by the Natal Parliament.

Later, Gandhi came personally to plead the cause of his fellow-settlers in South Africa, and toured the country, educating Indian public opinion. Among other places, Bombay heard an address from him on September 26, 1896. Pherozeshah presided, and, in introducing the lecturer, praised the great skill, pluck, ability and perseverance shown by the slim young man from Kathiawar, then unknown to fame, but whose mysticism and asceticism were to exercise in later years such a tremendous influence over his countrymen of all classes and creeds. A resolution was passed, authorizing the chairman to address the Secretary of State for India, soliciting his attention to the hardships and disabilities, under which

Her Majesty's Indian subjects in South Africa were labouring, as set forth in the various memorials presented on their behalf, and imploring him to take suitable measures for their redress.

In pursuance of that resolution, Pherozeshah submitted a lengthy representation to the Secretary of State, pointing out the harshness and injustice of the various measures which one State after another had adopted for the purpose of reducing to a position of helotry the settlers whose labour had contributed to the development of the country. The sheer iniquity of the whole thing needed no demonstration. A section at least of British public opinion was conscious of the responsibilities of the Imperial Government in the matter. *The Times,* in a series of powerful articles, championed the cause of the unhappy settlers in a manner which did it credit.

REFERENCES

1. Chintamani, C.Y., *Speeches and Writings of Sir Pherozeshah Mehta, op. cit.*, p. 406.
2. *Ibid.*, p. 163.
3. *Ibid.*, p. 164.
4. *Ibid.*
5. Speeches of Pherozeshah Mehta in the Bombay Town Hall on July 23, 1892.
6. Chintamani, C.Y., *Speeches and Writings of Sir Pherozeshah Mehta, op. cit.*, p. 637.
7. *Ibid.*, p. 49.
8. Mody, Homi, *Sir Pherozeshah Mehta, op. cit.*, p. 177.
9. *Ibid.*, p. 180.
10. *Ibid.*, pp. 184-185.
11. Mody, Homi, *Pherozeshah Mehta, op. cit.*, pp. 88-89.
12. *The Tribune* Lahore (Chandigarh), 30-01-1985.
13. *Ibid.*, 1 March, 1895.
14. Mody, Homi, *Pherozeshah Mehta, op. cit.*, pp. 92-93.
15. *Ibid.*, pp. 205-206.
16. *Ibid.*, pp. 100-101.

4

LOCAL SELF-GOVERNMENT

Various experiments in municipal government had been tried, but none of them had succeeded in ridding Bombay of her filth and dirt and general insanitation in the nineteenth century. There was a more or less complete absence of even the ordinary comforts of town life, let alone its amenities. There were no roads to speak of; only narrow and tortuous lanes and streets. Such markets and slaughter-houses as were to be found were centres for disseminating infection and disease. As regards the conservancy system, the scavenger was master of the situation, and was in a position to impose his own terms. Scarcity of water and outbreaks of epidemics like cholera and small-pox were more or less normal features of the city's life in those days.

It was under such conditions that the Act of 1865 came into being. It did away with the absurd system of administration by three commissioners, which had proved so disastrous, and vested the sole executive power in the hands of a single official, responsible to the Bench of justices. A Controller of Municipal Accounts was appointed to prevent abuse of authority by the Commissioner. The Justices of the Peace of the Town and Island of Bombay were constituted as a body corporate with a common seal, for there was no other representative body of men to whom municipal government could be entrusted.

The new regime was heir to a heavily burdened state. Nevertheless, a vast programme of improvements was undertaken by the Commissioner, Arthur Crawford, supported by his energetic assistant, Dr. Hewlett, the Health Officer. The years that followed witnessed strenuous activity in every direction. From being "one foul cesspool and sewers discharging on the sand,"[1] the city was made clean and healthy. The scavenger's tyranny was overthrown, and a sound conservancy system was established. Broad roads and foot-paths and adequate lighting arrangements were provided, and the citizens were no longer obliged to stumble in the dark along narrow and uneven lanes and thoroughfares. A satisfactory system of water supply was introduced, a market which was the envy of other towns was built, and open spaces were created in various centres. The old ramparts which surrounded the Fort had already been pulled down, a large area on the western foreshore had been reclaimed, and various other improvements had been effected under the inspiration of Sir Bartle Frere, the then Governor of Bombay, who saw in the Gateway of the East possibilities of development into one of the finest cities in the world. Mr. Crawford's vision no less broad, he laboured strenuously to bring Bombay in line with the most progressive towns in the West. What he accomplished is writ large in her history. His ways were autocratic, however, and his disregard of the financial aspect of his policy was truly sublime. He brushed aside all constitutional checks, and both the justices and the Controller of Accounts found themselves helpless before his masterful personality.

So long as things went well, this one-man-rule appeared to be free from objection, though not infrequently lively encounters took place between the Commissioner and his critics on the Bench of Justices. But the Municipality was soon on the verge of bankruptcy, and all the pent-up forces of discontent which had lain under the surface for several years burst out, and a loud outcry was raised for doing away with the obnoxious Commissioner and the Act which was supposed to be responsible for his autocracy. Public indignation was roused specially by the manner in which the taxes were collected. In the picturesque language of one of the stalwarts of that period, "the vocabulary of denunciation had been exhausted in characterising the present method of obtaining the Municipal income as one of the most iniquitous things the sun looks down upon, either in torrid or temperate zones."[2]

Various committees were appointed from time to time to consider this state of things, but this method of putting off the evil day, which seems to have been in fashion just as much in those un-regenerate days as in our own breathless times, did not prove very satisfactory. Ultimately, the justices were constrained to ask Government to appoint a commission to inquire into and report upon the administration of the Municipality and the changes which were necessary in its constitution. To this the Government replied by inquiring—and not without reason—whether the justices themselves could not, under the powers which they already possessed, secure a more complete control than they had hitherto exercised, over the masterful Commissioner. This somewhat tactless reply did not improve matters very much, and only resulted in further committees being appointed and a few more irregularities being brought to light. At length, an exasperated public decided to take matters into its own hands, and a Ratepayers' Association came into existence in November 1870. It lost no time in sending up a monster petition to the Bench of Justices, detailing the grievances of the public and asking for redress. The Bench pleaded helplessness, and the memorialists were consequently obliged to approach Government directly.

In the meantime, however, the more active spirits on the Bench decided to bring the issue to a head, and James Forbes, one of the leading merchants of the day, placing himself at the head of what may be called the Opposition, gave a notice of motion to have the constitution of the Municipality altered, so as to secure more effective control of the executive, and greater efficiency and economy of administration. A special meeting of the justices was called on the 30th June, 1871, in the *Durbar* room of the Town Hall to discuss the proposition. It was a memorable meeting in more ways than one. Unparalleled scenes of enthusiasm marked the occasion, and a procession with bands playing marched past the Town Hall to stimulate the zeal of the reformers. The entire Bombay, including his wife were present to watch the great struggle between the reformers and the champions of the Crawford regime.

The meeting was announced for three o'clock, but long before and long after that hour, Church Gate Street and Elphinstone Circle were crowded with vehicles of every description, all trending their way to the rendezvous at the Town Hall. The large room in which the meeting was held was full but still fresh crowds kept surging up to the doors—only to be informed by the constables that there was no space at all. The "oldest inhabitant" pronounced solemnly that there had never been such a meeting in his recollection.... Round a large table in the centre of the Hall, sat their worships on half a dozen rows of chairs, and the rest of the available space was packed with a dense mass of European and Native gentlemen in every variety of costume.[3]

Perhaps no other problem in the civic and political life of Bombay has brought together on one platform such a galaxy of talents as was evidenced on that memorable day in June. There were gathered at the meeting men distinguished in every walk of life, keen to serve the interests of the city they loved. Jamsetjee Jejeebhoy, Naoroji Furdunji, Sorabji Beagalee, Vishvanath Mandlik, Budrudin Tyabji, Pherozeshah Mehta, Dosabhoy Framji, Mahadeo Govind Ranade, Nafayen Wassudeo—such were among the representatives of the Indian community. The British element was represented by such notable men as Robert Knight, James Maclean, Martin Wood, James Forbes, Hamilton Maxwell, Captain Jiancock, Captain Henry, John Connon and Thomas Blaney. These were the makers of the new Bombay, the foundations of which had been laid during the epoch-making administration of Sir Bartle Frere. They were gathered that evening to fight the battle of municipal reform, and to lay broad and deep the foundations of local self-government in the city.

The debate was worthy of the occasion, and lasted through four sittings. An enthusiastic public applauded every telling hit, and spurred its champions to do their best. It is not necessary to enter into a discussion of the proposition moved by Forbes, and the several amendments thereto, which were proposed by both the apologists and the opponents of the redoubtable Commissioner, who gave and received many hard knocks in the course of the debate. The main feature of most of these proposals was the abolition of the commissionership, and the substitution in its place of an executive Town Council assisted by a Secretary. Considering the experience and capacity of the leaders in the movement, one cannot help a feeling of astonishment at the utter fatuity of this remedy for municipal mismanagement, for it was a revival in another form of the joint control, which had proved such a disastrous failure in the case of the Board of Conservancy and its successor, the triumvirate of municipal commissioners, who were in existence prior to 1865. There were, indeed, some members of the Bench who realized this, and were in fawour of retaining executive government in one single officer, but the proposals they put forward lacked the broad outlook and grasp of essentials, without which all reforms were mere tinkering with the problem.

It was given to one man alone out of that large and representative body to lay his finger with unerring instinct on the weak spot in the municipal administration, and boldly to point out the right remedy. It was Pherozeshah who stood up in his place towards the end of that long and historic debate, and confidently told the justices how they had all failed to grasp the real point at issue, and had been led away into reviving discredited schemes in a desperate endeavour to get out of their existing difficulties.[4] The proposals he put forward, and which were ultimately embodied in the Act of 1872, reveal a political sagacity and breadth of outlook, which for a young man of twenty-six may well be considered astonishing, particularly when we remember that he was propounding principles which were but dimly realized even by the ablest among his colleagues. But it was a distinguishing characteristic of Pherozeshah even at that early age that he could see further than any of his contemporaries, and possessed the shrewdness of judgement which was truly remarkable. His receptive mind had imbibed, besides, in the free atmosphere of England, ideas and principles of government which the writings of political philosophers like Mill had made current coin. He had also studied the working of self-governing institutions in the very home of political and civic freedom.

It was, therefore, with much confidence that Pherozeshah placed before his older and more experienced colleagues on the Bench of justices his views on the question of municipal reform. After pointing out how the proposals of Messrs. Forbes and Naoroji

Furdunji regarding an executive Town Council were radically unsound, he proceeded to show how even those amendments which recognized this had failed to touch the real cause of the breakdown of the system. In Pherozeshah's opinion, it was not the Act of 1865 that was at fault so much as thc constitution of the body which was charged with the administration of municipal affairs. "There never will be," he observed, "efficient municipal administration in Bombay, till there is a popular and responsible Bench of justices elected at regular intervals by the ratepayers themselves, a consultative Town Council elected out of it, with a responsible executive officer at its head, appointed by Government, and a Controller of Accounts appointed by the Bench to control the Commissioner."[5] The speaker was aware that most people scouted the idea as absurd and visionary, and one, which in any case, would never be entertained by Government. As to the last objection, he ventured to say that the time was past when strong popular opinion on any subject could be successfully resisted by Government for any length of time. And as for the feasibility of the proposal to set up an elective body, he contented himself with a quotation from a notable speech made by Anstey at a gathering of the East India Association, in which that versatile and erratic genius had pointed out that local self-government in the widest acceptation of the term was as old as the East itself. Pherozeshah wound up by declaring that only in such a bold and decisive measure as he had outlined, were to be found real salvation and efficiency, and that for that reason, he was unable to agree with any of the palliatives proposed by Forbes and other members of the Bench. The speech, able and impressive as it was, met with a somewhat cold reception; for people were in no mood than to listen to original suggestions. They were all out to denounce the Commissioner and the Act, which was supposed to be responsible for his financial vagaries.

This memorable debate on municipal reform came to an end on the fourth day amidst scenes of enthusiasm. The net result of the half a dozen resolutions moved during the discussion and the twenty-six speeches which were delivered, was a representation to Government to appoint a commission of inquiry, and to take necessary action in the light of the various reports which had been made from time to time, and the resolutions which had been passed at the meeting. Government, thereupon, appointed a committee under the chairmanship of Sir Theodore Hope to inquire into the financial position of the Municipality. The report of the committee revealed grave irregularities, which led to a recurrence of the agitation. Again Forbes took the lead, and addressed a representation to Government asking them to relieve the municipality of its embarrassments, and to set up a system of administration on sounder and more progressive lines.

It was about this time, when the agitation was at its highest, and was being conducted on both sides with extreme rancour and violence, that Pherozeshah decided to place his views on municipal government once more before the public. He regarded the question as one of general interest, and was anxious it should be discussed by a wider public than that before which he had laid his proposals on the first occasion. A meeting of the Bombay Branch of the East India Association was arranged, and on the 29th November, 1871, Pherozeshah read his paper on the "Municipal Reform Question" at the Framji Cowasji Institute before a large audience. The chair was taken by Dosabhoy Framji, who, in his opening remarks, observed that he had no doubt it would be a pleasant evening, and that the lessons they might learn would be useful and instructive. How very pleasant the evening was going to be, the chairman was soon to realize.

The paper was an elaborate and detailed exposition of the views Pherozeshah had already propounded at the Town Hall meeting. After pointing out that Forbes and his supporters had allowed their zeal to overrun their discretion with the confidence of youth, he preached to his audience a homily on the duty of those who would aspire to lead their fellow-men. Said he:

"The self-constituted leaders of popular movements have a two-fold duty to perform. It is not sufficient for them to stand forth boldly to give loud utterance to the confused and incoherent popular cries. It is not sufficient for them to reiterate and proclaim the popular indiscriminate wailings and inconclusive analyses of the public grievances. There is another and a higher duty cast upon them, the duty of guiding and rolling the movement in its proper path, of extricating it from the confusion of words and thoughts under which it usually labours, of analysing the genuine and substantial causes of it, of discussing and proposing measures well adapted to meet the end in view."[6]

After criticizing the attitude of the leaders of the reform movement, Pherozeshah entered upon a vigorous defence of Crawford, and showed what vast improvements had been effected during his strenuous regime. He pictured to his audience the woeful condition of Bombay as the Commissioner had found her in 1865. It was not a time for patient deliberation, but for prompt and vigorous action "....there is a crisis in human affairs when ordinary means avail not, when men must consent to strong measures on the sole condition that they are efficient, when they must give up their freedom and lay aside their most cherished institutions, their most valued forms and guarantees of order and economy, and submit to the strong rule and the strong hand, absolute and arbitrary, on the sole condition that it fails not. Such crises are common in the history of the growth of minor institutions as of great states and commonwealths."[7]

The hour had found the man, and Pherozeshah thought it was highly unjust that the great work done by Crawford for the city should be allowed to be altogether obscured by the financial irregularities of which he was undoubtedly guilty. It was also a muddled view of the situation to saddle the Act with the sole responsibility for the unfortunate position of affairs in which the Municipality had found itself placed. If passion and prejudice had not perverted the public mind, he continued, it would have been realized that the fault lay in nothing so much as in the constitution of the body charged with the function of enforcing the provisions of the Act. Elected by Government for life, the Bench of Justices was by the very conditions of its existence, organized only for inefficiency and incompetency. It was not their fault, for, as John Bright once said of the Board of Directors of the East India Company, the Justices would be expected to act just about as well as any other equal number of persons elected by the same process, standing under the same circumstances, and surrounded by the same difficulties.

The real remedy, Pherozeshah went on to point out, lay in the introduction of the free representative principle in the constitution of the municipal body. A careful study of Indian history showed conclusively that there was no racial or radical incapacity on the part of Indians for enjoying representative institutions. Village communities existed in India from very ancient times, and within their own sphere they used to exercise wide powers. There was ample testimony to the competence with which they discharged their functions. It was, therefore, absurd to suggest that representative institutions were altogether foreign to the genius of the people of India. Equally fallacious and contrary to the teachings of History, was to say that they were out of place in a system of government which was paternal in character. From these and other considerations, it was obvious that a measure of local self-government could safely be established, particularly in Bombay, where her citizens had given ample proof of their capacity and public spirit. Unless such a constitutional reform was brought about, it would be idle to expect any improvement in civic affairs. The changes proposed by Mr. Forbes and others were against all principle and experience, and were a revival in another form of experiments, which had failed disastrously in the past.

The views expounded by Pherozeshah in this paper may be read with profit today, not only for their lucid and vigorous exposition of first principles, but also as illustrating the maturity of thought, his political sagacity which characterized the man even at that early age. The audience, however, was in no mood to appreciate the point of view of the lecturer, or the ability with which he had marshalled his facts and arguments. Blinded by passion and prejudice, it strongly resented his daring attempt to place the administration of Crawford in a proper perspective. It did not want any defence of the obnoxious Commissioner, and it conveyed its displeasure at the attempt in a forcible manner. Great disorder prevailed during the continuance of the lecture, and uproarious scenes marked its conclusion. As the following account will show, the proceedings were of a very lively character, and terminated amidst scenes of wild confusion:

"Mr. Pherozeshah then ascended the platform and began his paper. His introductory remarks elicited a few 'hear, hears' which stood out in bold relief against one or two vigorous hisses which seemed thrown in by some persons of taste, in order that the value of the slight applause should be increased rather than drowned, and the sounds rendered more sweet by the additional charm of contrast." The lecturer however continued, through the short, sharp staccatoed hiss which marked every full stop, and which ultimately warned us of where the very commas occurred, was still sent forth with exemplary vigour and enthusiasm. Scarcely, however, had each of these gentle reminders of disapproval been uttered, then it had to do battle with an ocean of other cries of 'shame, share, insulting,' mostly disputing its authority, and amongst which it soon expired. At length the paper was finished, when the dissatisfaction which was felt by many members became evident, whilst others, desirous of carrying on matters peaceably, cried 'order, order, chair, chair,' but to no purpose. The steam had been raised to too high a pressure, and it was absolutely necessary to blow off a quantity, and in this operation all sense of order and regulation seemed to be lost sight of. Sorabji Rustomji Bunsha rose and attempted to say a few words. The chairman rose, and he also attempted to say a few words, and it was too evident that others were longing to follow his example. The chairman, finding a great obstacle in the way of his addressing the meeting in the person of Sorabji, who was carrying on matters very enthusiastically in another quarter, requested that gentleman to be seated—an argument, the force of which however that gentleman seemed unable to see—but as he faced the chairman evidently desiring to be convinced on the subject before he could give place to another. Dosabhoy took the opportunity of the momentary pause of proposing an adjournment. 'Adjournment, adjournment,' responded those on the chairman's left. 'Hear him, hear him,' answered those on the right. Again the chairman attempted to make himself heard, but as by this time Sorabji was well launched, and in full swing, the expressions of indignation which escaped him were rendered no more intelligible. Each moment the confusion increased, till the whole meeting row, as if by one accord, and each person began to raise his voice in defence of the party they considered in the right. Even in this, one might have heard the opinions of those who were pressing close to him, had it not been for the vigorous expedient which occurred to some, of laying into the tables with their walking canes, right merrily. This, however, was eventually stopped by the gas being turned out just as the second chairman (Dosabhoy having stated that the meeting was adjourned and left) was about to take his seat. This had the effect of causing parties to see that they were really, all in the dark, which it would have required many hours' talking to do.[8]

Thus ended the "pleasant" evening of which the hopeful chairman had spoken in his introductory remarks. But the storm provoked by the fearless expression of such unconventional and unpopular opinions as abounded in the lecture did not easily subside. *The Times of India,* one of the most trenchant critics of the Crawford regime, while regretting that the disorder which prevailed at the meeting prevented the exposure of the "thundering mistake" that all improvements effected in Bombay since 1865 were, due to the late Commissioner, went on to observe reference to Pherozeshah:

"But that gentleman may thank himself for the disorder that occurred. It is all very well to claim tolerance for differences of opinion, but it is wasting time and patience for anyone to thrust before the public sentiments and pleas that have already been disposed of by full debate. Life is too short, and the world too long to place its time at the disposal of ingenious or inconsiderate gentlemen like Pherozeshah, who for the mere sake of debate strive to persuade men against the evidence of their senses. We had not the excitement, pleasurable or tedious, of listening to the paper in question, nor have we had the opportunity of perusing it, though it is in print, but we are quite satisfied with the accounts given of it, from which we infer that, excepting a few paragraphs, it is a peculiarly perverse, erroneous and sophistical production."[9]

The article ended by expressing surprise and regret that the lecture should have been allowed by the committee of the Association to be read at the general meeting. That this was also the general feeling of the members of that body was made clear by subsequent proceedings. A requisition signed by about thirty members was sent to the chairman, asking him to call a special general meeting to consider the desirability of expunging the paper read by Pherozeshah from the records of the Association. A meeting was accordingly convened on the 18th December in the Framji Cowasji Institute. Dr. Bhau Daji was in the chair, and there was a large audience. Pherozeshah was present but walked out with one or two of his friends, shortly after the commencement of the proceedings, followed by a "tempest of hisses, varied by shouts of 'Order, Order,' and vigorous hurrahs." The proposition for expunging the lecture from the record was carried by a large majority, and the chairman wound up the proceedings by declaring that the paper was to be considered "as not read and as not worth discussion," and by apologizing for the incident, and assuring the public that there would be no recurrence of it in the future![10]

It was one of the most characteristic incidents in the career of Pherozeshah. It was at once a measure of his strength of character and political acumen. Few men would have ventured at his age to put forward views so utterly unpopular, and so greatly in advance of his times. But he possessed courage in a remarkable degree, and once his mind was made up on any question, he, expressed himself with uncompromising independence, undeterred either by popular opinion or official displeasure.

Ridiculed and abused, as most men who are ahead of their times, he had ultimately the satisfaction of seeing the broad lines of the constitution he had chalked out adopted in the Municipal Act of 1872. Under that constitution worked by some of the best minds in the city, its administration had made remarkable progress in every direction. With the lapse of time, however, the necessity for a more uniform and progressive enactment was felt, and ever since the publication of Lord Ripon's memorable resolution on local self-government, the Corporation had made various representations to Government from time to time, in the drawing up of which Pherozeshah had taken a leading part.

After various schemes had been discussed and rejected, including a draft Bill providing for a system of executive committees, which was referred to the Corporation for criticism, and which that body condemned as a reversion to an unsound principle, Government introduced the long-looked for Bill in the Legislative Council on 16 July, 1887. It was the result of the joint labours; of Naylor the Legal Remembrancer, and Mr. (afterwards Sir) Charles Ollivant, the Municipal Commissioner, who, during his temporary absence in England in 1883, had been deputed by the Corporation to study the systems of municipal government in existence in Great Britain. In the Council, the only Indian of outstanding merit, before the Bill was introduced, was Telang, and to strengthen the popular element on that body, and to secure the requisite knowledge and experience of civic affairs, the Government of Lord Reay had the wisdom to appoint Pherozeshah as an "additional" member. The appointment was received on all sides with cordial approval. *The Bombay Gazette* spoke of it as "a very appropriate recognition of ability shown in many fields," and particularly referred to Pherozeshah's moderation and independence. *The Indian Spectator,* conducted by the late B.M. Malabari, a journalist and social reformer of considerable note, was equally appreciative. "In Mr. P.M. Mehta, the Bombay Government secures for its Legislative Council a worthy man. His talents, breadth of views, and public spirit make him one of the best native members the Bombay Council has had."[11]

The Bill in the shape in which it was introduced was in many respects of a retrograde character. It sought to enlarge the authority of the Commissioner at the expense of the Corporation, and it reserved to Government powers of initiative and interference in various matters, which ought rightly to fall within the province of a local body. Strangely enough, the men responsible for this illiberal measure were not reactionaries in any sense. At the head of the administration was a Governor who had come with the reputation of a man of wide culture and sympathies. The official sponsor of the Bill, Naylor, was a just and fair-minded civilian, open to conviction, and without the prejudices of his caste. And yet, the measure, evolved after years of consideration and criticism, lacked the essentials of a satisfactory scheme of local self-government. The fact was that the original framework was that of Ollivant, who could not entirely divest himself of the point of view of the class to which he belonged, and in the Bill submitted to the Council, the principal features of his scheme had been retained. Naylor claimed for the Bill, that it was designed "to secure to the citizens of Bombay the greatest possible efficiency in municipal service with the most complete possible control over expenditure." Telang, on the other hand, pronounced it to be "a retrograde measure, so retrograde, indeed, that if on voting I had to make my choice merely between this Bill and the old law, I should unhesitatingly give my voice in favour of the law as it at present exists, with all its anomalies, its laxities of phraseology and its conflicts of jurisdiction."[12]

Such was the character of the Bill when it was referred to a Select Committee, consisting of Sir Maxwell Melville, a member of the Executive Council and once a distinguished judge of the High Court, the Advocate-General, Macpherson, and Messrs. Telang, Pherozeshah and Kazi Shahabudin. The Committee conducted its deliberations on the cool heights of Mahabaleshwar, where the official mind is said to derive strength and elasticity which are supposed to be impossible in the burning plains. Evidently, Pherozeshah was not in a hurry to enjoy the privilege of deliberating on affairs of state on a hill-top, for late in October we find a telegram from the Secretary to the Legislative Council, informing him that the meetings of the Committee depended entirely on his arrival. When he went, he found that in the absence of Telang, the brunt of the fighting was to be borne by him. His official colleagues were fair-minded men, on the whole, but they had their prejudices and prepossessions, and their acquaintance with the practical working of the Municipal Act was slight. Their conversion to the popular view on many points of importance was brought about by the exercise of much tact, patience and ability on the part of Pherozeshah. He was greatly assisted by the large measure of criticism to which the Bill was subjected in public, and in particular, by a very elaborate exposition of its views which the Corporation had forwarded to Government.

Perhaps, the most important incident in which the measure was improved was that whereby the municipal government of the city was vested in the Corporation, subject to express provisions in the Act. The original clause had set up the Commissioner as the authority charged with carrying out the provisions of the statute had sought to place him in a position in which he would have the conduct of affairs, and constituted himself the principal authority in matters of local self-government. Telang had objected to the clause on the first reading and had rightly characterized it as the key note of the Bill. Its alteration, therefore, was a matter of importance and purged the measure of its most objectionable feature.

To the part played by Pherozeshah in bringing about this other modification, his life-long friend and colleague Dinshaw Wacha, has borne a testimony which will not be regarded as exaggerated:

"His patient, persevering and convincing advocacy of the amendments after amendments which he proposed were principally, nay, almost wholly, instrumental in casting the Bill in an entirely different shape from that in which it had been originally moulded by Naylor. Of this colossal labour, this expenditure of time and mental energy of a very high order, the public have little or no knowledge. He had the largest share of all his other colleagues in modifying each and all of the original sections."[13]

The result of the Select Committee's deliberations was to liberalize the Bill in many important particulars. Several features of it were still open to objection, and the Corporation took up a strong position with regard to them. In the course of a fresh representation it made on the subject, it observed:

"The Corporations are anxious that their view of the case should not be ignored; either they are, or they are not, to be the governing body of this city. If they are to be the governing body, they should be entrusted with full powers to carry out what they believe to be right and best; if they are not to be the governing body, there is then no apparent necessity for their existence."[14]

This bold statement of the case was worthy of the Corporation of those days, consisting as it did of representatives of the people noted for their ability and strength of character, and of a strong and independent body of Europeans who served the city with singular zeal and devotion. When the second reading of the Bill was taken up on 7 March, 1888, the ground was fought inch by inch, and most of the modifications which the Select Committee had thrown out were adopted. Mr. Naylor led off with an utterance indicative of the conciliatory attitude of himself and his official colleagues. He was followed by Pherozeshah in a speech which students of municipal politics might read with profit even at the present day. He traced the history of the municipal government in the city, in order to show that the Bill, as originally introduced, was a retrograde measure and was calculated to put back the hands of the clock. The Select Committee had altered it a great deal, but there still remained several objectionable features which would have to be strenuously resisted in the Council. For instance, there was a section, which proposed to give very wide powers to the Commissioner in cases of emergency. There was another provision for authorizing the appointment of a Deputy Commissioner, to which Pherozeshah was strongly opposed as leading to divided responsibility. Barring these and a few other obnoxious clauses, he readily recognised that the Bill constituted a substantial measure of advance along the road to local self-government.

It is unnecessary to do more than dip into the pages which record the long and often interesting discussions which took place in the Council when the Bill was considered section by section. To those interested in the subject, a study of Dinshaw Wacha's graphic history of municipal institutions in Bombay may be confidently recommended. It gives the salient points of the long-drawn debates in the Council, and vividly portrays the parts played by individual members. For our purpose, it is enough to say that many of the objectionable features, which still dung to the Bill when it emerged from the Select Committee, were removed by the strenuous efforts of Pherozeshah and Telang, ably backed by Sir Frank Forbes Adam, one of the most liberal-minded merchant princes of the day.

The result was due in part also to the very fair attitude which was adopted by Lord Reay, a genuine lover of freedom, and by the official spokesmen who piloted the Bill through the Council. We have, in consequence, in the Act of 1888, a close approximation to the ideal of municipal government cherished by Telang, namely, "a strong executive responsible to the Corporation, and an enlightened Corporation watchful over its executive."[15] Those who assisted in bringing about the desired consummation might well have been proud of their handiwork. It was not, of course, free from defects, but it was as perfect as the conflicting forces of conservatism on the one hand and radicalism on the other could make it. As Sir Raymond, then Mr. West, observed, there were very few occasions on which a Bill of such complexity and involving the balancing of so many principles, which at the first seemed more or less opposed, had been passed through a Legislative Council with such general approval of its proposals. The man whose opinion on the subject most counted was well pleased with it. On the third reading of the Bill, Pherozeshah characterized it as an eminently workable and practicable measure. It was drawn on sound principles—sound in theory and tested by long experience. It had carefully steered clear of two pitfalls. On the one hand, it had avoided the blunder of making the Commissioner anything more than the executive officer of the supreme administrative body, which was the Corporation. On the other, it had resisted the temptation of abolishing the Commissioner in favour of executive committees or councils, or of changing the mode of his appointment.

Lord Reay wound up the proceedings with a lucid exposition of the fundamental principles underlying the proposed legislation. Bombay owes much to this courageous statesman, who laboured during five strenuous years to give her a pure and progressive administration. While we recall with gratitude the part played by her sons in securing for her a genuine measure of self-government, let us not forget that the man who presided over her fortunes at an important juncture was imbued with liberal principles, which he was anxious to translate into practice. He set the tone to the Council and the debates throughout maintained a high level of ability, moderation and good sense. His summary of the main features of the Bill was admirable in its lucidity:

"Government has mainly had in view to give through this Bill to the ratepayers the greatest security against extravagance and a wasteful administration. Representatives of the city are responsible for the good government of the city. A number of duties are imposed on them which it would be impossible for them in their corporate capacity to fulfil in detail. They are obviously a deliberative assembly, and the result of their deliberations will naturally assume the shape of bye-laws, resolutions or instructions, the execution of which must be left to another authority. Their constitution prohibits the performance of administrative duties which no representative assembly in any other country has ever dreamt of undertaking. They, like all other legislative assemblies, influence, control and direct the administration by giving or withholding the funds for certain purposes, but they are not and cannot be administrative bodies. The same Act of the Legislature which creates them must, therefore, create other authorities for the purpose of carrying out the duties which the legislative and superintending body cannot execute."[16]

Lord Keay did not fail to pay a tribute to those who had worked with him in a spirit of wholehearted co-operation. He gave due praise to Sir Charles Ollivant for the labour and thought he had devoted to the drafting of the Bill, and to Naylor, Latham and Macpherson, who had throughout been most helpful in piloting it through the Council. He spoke appreciatively of Telang's services, and last, but not least, he bore generous testimony to the value of Pherozeshah's guidance and co-operation:

"I appointed the Honourable Mr. Mehra on this Council, so that we might have the benefit of his intimate knowledge of municipal affairs in the Select Committee in our debates. The honourable member has taken a considerable share in facilitating the passage and improvements of this Bill which, I believe, meets his views, which, I take it, are representative of those of the community, though, I may be permitted to add, his views were characterized by that independence of judgment which marks a representative as distinct from a delegate."[17]

With this graceful compliment, we may bring to an end this brief narrative of a legislative measure which has given Bombay the inestimable boon of a sound and progressive municipal administration, which has been regarded as a model for the whole country. It is still a long way behind Western municipalities, both as regards its administrative achievements and its conception of the functions of a civic corporation, But for all that, the Act of 1888 has given the citizens of Bombay a charter of local self-government, which has proved the most successful, as it has been the first experiment of its kind in India. It has stood the test of time, and, subject to a few modifications which experience has rendered necessary, has been found to be an eminently sound and workable measure, which has provided an excellent training ground for the development of administrative capacity.

REFERENCES

1. Mody, Homi, *Sir Pherozeshah Mehta, op. cit.*, p. 34.
2. *Ibid.*, p. 35.
3. *The Times of India*, 6-7-1931.
4. Sastri, V. S. Srinivasa, *Life and Times of Sir Pherozeshah Mehta, op. cit.*, p. 110.
5. *Ibid.*
6. Mody, Homi, *Sir Pherozeshah Mehta, op. cit.*, p. 40.
7. *Ibid.*
8. *The Bombay Gazette*, 1-12-1871.
9. *The Times of India*, 10-12-1871.
10. Mody, Homi, *Pherozeshah Mehta, op. cit.*, p. 32.
11. Mody, Homi, *Sir Pherozeshah Mehta, op. cit.*, p. 109.
12. *Ibid.*
13. Wacha, D.E., Introduction, *Speeches and Writings of Sir Pherozeshah Mehta,* Allahabad: The Indian Press, 1905, p. 19.
14. *Ibid.*
15. Ibid.
16. Ibid., p. 20.
17. Mody, Homi, *Sir Pherozeshah Mehta, op. cit.*, pp. 113-14.

5

MEHTA AND GOKHALE

Pherozeshah was many years senior to Gokhale; twenty-one years is the difference between them; and that partly determines the attitude of the junior. It was one of respect and admiration. This attitude never changed throughout their lives, and throughout their association in the work of the country. Pherozeshah and Gokhale resembled each other in many qualities which we value. They had burning love for the country, they had earnestness, they had courage, they had industry, and they had profound knowledge of the conditions of India and her people. They both worked in exalted spheres; and their work has the common characteristics or lasting value and inspiring patriotism. Pherozeshah conquered you almost the moment he said, "I love you". So did Gokhale. But they did it in very different ways. In the words of Rt. V.S. Srinivas Sastra, "There was in the look of either, not merely beauty, but impressiveness of character. You felt that they were men to know whom was to receive a great influence in your life. You felt at once that both were above all other countrymen of theirs, in the extent of their knowledge and in the extent of their influence. But I must say at once that their attraction differed greatly. Sir Pherozeshah seemed to dominate you. When you saw him full in the face, there was a squint in his eyes which fixed you almost. You felt that you were in his power. I have seen him in the Legislative Council speak with authority and with vigour, that drew everybody's attention to him; and I have seen how, when any member of the Council spoke, every two minutes or three minutes he used to turn to know what impression he was producing on this master of the House. I cannot say that Gokhale's authority shone to the same extent on his face. He captivated you also; but there was a pleasingness, if I may say so, in his look, a brotherliness, and lovingness, a tenderness almost of familiarity which drew you to him with a bond of affection. But there the similarity ends."[1] Sir Pherozeshah had a rich and sonorous voice; when he spoke to an audience, he could be heard in the most distant corner. Even his whispers did not fail to catch your attention. His diction was dignified and powerful; and when he chose to criticise people, he hit hard. If he was against a person, there was no mercy in the way he handled him. He could be rough as well as gentle. And there was a wide range of voice, which Gokhale utterly lacked. Gokhale spoke also so as to command the attention of his hearers, but his voice was different; it was pitched in a lower key. When, one heard him, one felt drawn to a person who spoke with his full heart, and meant every word of what he said and every syllable of every word that he uttered. One could see sincerity and conviction stamped on his features and in his voice, there was no banter; there was no ridiculing of the adversary; there was nothing like hitting hard. There was argument piled upon argument; there was reasoning; large number of statistics were from registers and returns, and above all there was a note of mild controversy and of persuasion, which was that of a friend, of a man who meant to convert to his opinion, and not of a person who desired to bear one down with authority or confound anyone with subtle reason.

Then there was in their personalities a wide difference that an observer could not help noticing. Pherozeshah came every day to his chambers and sat there, with a number of admirers gathered round him, a small faithful band who never failed him, but stood loyally by their master, obedient to his call and breathing the same sentiments as he did. It was, as it were, a levee that he held every morning in his chambers. One could see about ten people, sometimes fifteen, but they were there always talking about matters of public importance, talking about the Bombay Corporation, talking about the great friends of India in this country and in Great Britain, talking about what mattered vitally to the country. When he came to an assembly, such as the Indian National Congress, all eyes were directed to where he sat. Nothing could go wrong so long as

Pherozeshah was awake and had the strings in his hands. He had a commanding personality, a personality which nobody could ignore.

Same cannot be said about Gokhale was not even nearly so and did not carry the same authority. In fact, in Gokhale's bearing and general attitude, there was a touch of shrinking and modesty, a disinclination to put himself forward. In fact in Gokhale's composition there was a great element of reverence. Towards his elders, towards those who were in the service of the country worth, towards those who had done any public service mentioning, towards those who not merely in age but in patriotism and character rose above the ordinary being towards these Gokhale never failed to show personal respect. Therefore, Gokhale in his attitude towards Dadabhai Naoroji, towards Ranade, towards Mehta, and even towards Mahatma Gandhi who was his junior by about four years, and towards all where he thought respect and reverence were due, he yielded them from his very soul.[2]

It was said that towards the latter part of his life, Sir Pherozeshah felt a kind of aloofness with Gokhale, as he felt that he was catching the ear of the country, that he was making a mark and that a rival was assuming importance over him. But this is not true. Neither of them by character or by conduct gave the smallest reason for the spread of such an idea. Sir Pherozeshah had established himself so securely and so unshakably in the heart of his countrymen, that envy of any kind was out of question. And so far as Gokhale was concerned, the idea of rivalry or eclipsing Sir Pherozeshah could never have taken shape in his simple and adoring heart. His was a noble soul; and to speak of him as trying to usurp the name or affection of another, is to do wrong to him. Gokhale himself wrote a letter to Sir Pherozeshah in 1901, after he had resigned from the Imperial Council. Gokhale who had been just elected to the local Legislative Council, wrote in his letter:

"I am about to retire from the Fergusson College to which I have dedicated the best years of my youth, and I intend to devote the rest of my life to political work in India and in England. I feel that unless young men come forward to devote all their time and energies to public work in the spirit in which Mr. Dadabhai Naoroji has been working for fifty years, not only is much real progress possible but even the ground which has been already gained is in danger of being lost. My wife's death has destroyed the principal tie which bound me to family life and settled home; and I can now carry without much effort into the field of politics the devotion with which I have been working for my college. I have built up for myself a small income of about Rs. 125 a month which, with my monthly pension of Rs. 20 from the College, is enough to keep me in comfort. What I want now is a chance of making myself useful to my country. Of course, everyone will be sincerely pleased if you continue to represent Bombay in the Supreme Council as long as health and energy are vouchsafed to you. Your great talents and unique record place you absolutely beyond the reach of competition. But it is rumoured, you are going shortly to retire from the Council. On personal grounds I should wish the resignation to come later.

"I was hoping that you would, even, if you did not stand for a fresh election at any rate complete your present term, which does not expire till the middle of 1902, that during the time I might, show some useful work in the local Council, so that when you retired you might consider me as not quite the least deserving among those who are working for public good in this presidency at a good and respectful distance behind you. Everyone feels—I state what I honestly think—that on the score of gifts, natural and acquired, on the score of prestige, on the score of those numerous qualities which are indispensable in a political leader, there is no equalling you or even coming near you.

"The same cannot be said, of course, of the men who aspire to succeed you, and there being little difference between the qualifications of the various candidates, I ask for your sympathy and encouragement. I am conscious I am too young for the position but the fierce mental anguish which I have had to endure since 1897 has made me older in judgement and experience. In any case it is not wholly a disadvantage that I shall begin the new career at a comparatively early age. I beg to assure you it is no mere personal ambition which is urging me to seek the honour. My reasons are different.

"In 1897, when a perfect storm of fierce criticism broke over my head in connection with my unhappy share in the incidents of that year, nothing wounded me deeper than Bhowanuggree's denunciation of me in the House of Commons as a 'despicable perjurer'. The words burnt into my heart and the night I read them, I made up my mind to devote my life as soon as I was free from my pledge, to the furtherance of our political cause in England, to which I had, without meaning it, done such serious injury. And for this work a brief period of membership of the Viceregal Council will be very useful. The painful affair of 1897 will perhaps be brought against me again and again, but the testimony of Lord Sandhurst himself and my membership of the Bombay and Supreme Councils subsequent to that incident, will go a long way towards silencing my critics. The English work is dear to my heart also for the reason that it will please Sir W. Wedderburn, Mr. Hume, and Mr. Dadabhai on whom I was instrumental in bringing humiliation four years ago. I have written frankly and without reserve, and hope I shall not be misunderstood. I already owe much to you in public life and I feel I may lay bare to you the aspirations as well at the wounds of my heart without being repulsed for doing so."[3]

Next year, there was the Report of the famous Raleigh Commission on Universities, published at the bidding of Lord Curzon, which created a violent agitation, throughout the country. The University bodies felt that there was danger in their recommendations and the Bombay Senate was the earliest to take account of the danger, and appointed a committee to consider the recommendations that Sir Raleigh had made. Sir Pherozeshah took a leading part in examining these recommendations minutely, and he was instrumental in getting a committee, composed of both Europeans and Indians unanimously to pass a report which was, to say the least, strongly critical of their recommendations and their tendencies. Gokhale knew well that although there was a violent feeling of hostility to the recommendations, it was not possible to get the University Committee to do likewise. They were divided. Sir Pherozeshah was to impose himself on the others, and produce a report which could be said to combat Lord Curzon's intentions to officialise the University (that was the word). Gokhale wrote:

"That you should have got the European Members of the Committee to join in all your criticisms and proposals, except one, is a remarkable triumph for us all; and everybody must recognise that it has been achieved mainly owing to your great tact and influence and your powerful personality. It is felt here that, if the Bombay Senate adopt & this report, as most probably will now be the case, the opposition to the Commission's recommendations will be enormously strengthened. They have no hope here of getting their own Senate to condemn the Report as ours has done, or rather will shortly do, and the difference in caliber and political grit between their leaders and ours is, therefore, at present being freely recognised here. You know how emotional these people are, and how easily swayed. The very men who, after the Congress of 1901, were violent in their denunciation of your and Mr. Bannerji's high-handedness in extinguishing Nundy's Indian Congress Committee, are now praising you to the skies and recognising in you—very justly—the greatest political leader of India in our time."[4]

Gokhale was in Madras in 1904 and spoke on the political situation. Gokhale then said about Sir Pherozeshah:

"This then is the lesson we have to learn from Japan (Japan was not then thought of as a possible enemy. The whole world admired Japan, and we all liked to know everything about Japan) that if our work is to be successful, our efforts cannot be concentrated unless leaders received from followers that disciplined obedience that you find in Japan. It is true that we have not got many single-minded leaders in the country to lead us, but we are not wholly without them. We have one such man in Sir Pherozeshah Mehta, darnest and patriotic, possessing high abilities, and qualified in every way to lead the country. But these men must receive more implicit support from the bulk of our educated men."[5]

Three years later there occurred a remarkable agitation in Bombay city. Sir Pherozeshah who had established his ascendancy in that Corporation beyond all dispute became the object of envy and jealousy to the European community there, who had resolved to band themselves together and unitedly bring their whole influence to bear on the electorate, so that Pherozeshah at the next opportunity may not be elected to the Corporation at all. Well, it was known that the party against Pherozeshah was led mainly by the officials of Government of Bombay—disgraceful to that Government, which is most shameful to recall at the present time. The important men of the Corporation, the Accountant-General, the Collector of Bombay and the Police Commissioner banded themselves together and openly canvassed the electorate called the Justices of the Peace. These exalted people had to elect sixteen persons, and the influence of the Accountant-General and the Collector and the Police Commissioner and other people was so great that it was possible for them to manipulate the polling that when the votes were counted, Pherozeshah would come seventeenth in the list. Luckily his keen eyes discovered that one of the sixteen was a contractor in the Bombay Corporation, and that he was not qualified to be elected at all. So in a trice, that man was displaced and Pherozeshah got in. But that is another matter. The fact that there was a movement by the leading Europeans backed by the *Times of India* and by other papers who had risen against this great leader and had banded themselves together and tried to get this man out of the Corporation, which was proud to call itself his child, and very often postponed its business if he was not able to attend, drew the attention of the whole country at that time. An enormous public meeting was held and it was felt that Gokhale who was then in Calcutta, doing his duties as member of the Imperial Council, should be summoned to be the Chairman of this meeting. He came and was received with great ovation as the man in India, who could voice the feelings of indignation and resentment, that were prevalent in the city of Bombay. I quote a passage from his speech the whole speech:

"A man with the great, transcendental abilities of Sir Pherozeshah Mehta, placing those abilities freely and unreservedly at the disposal of his City for nearly 40 years, is bound to attain a position of unrivalled predominance in any Corporation and in any country. That such a man should tower head and shoulders above his fellowmen after such a record is only to be expected, and those who complain of this quarrel with the very elements, of our human nature. Such predominance implies deep gratitude on the part of those to whose service a great career has been consecrated, joined to that profound confidence in the wisdom and judgement of the leader, which goes with such gratitude. Pherozeshah's position in the Corporation is no doubt without a parallel in India; but there is a close parallel to it in the mighty influence exercised by Mr. Chamberlain at Birmingham, and it is not dissimilar to the position occupied by Lord Palmerston for many years in Whig, England, and later by the great Gladstone in the counsels of the Liberal Party."[6]

The next letter read is testimony of a kind which cannot be impeached. It was not written to Pherozeshah, and it was not uttered at a public meeting. It is a private letter written to V. Krishnaswami Aiyer in 1908. The Reforms proposed to be introduced by Lord Minto were expected to be announced in time for the 1908 Congress, the first official Congress held in this very city, Madras. Gokhale had laboured hard, along with Lord Minto, to give these Reforms liberal shape and a progressive character. He was very proud of the part he had taken in them and he wrote to V. Krishnaswami Aiyer a letter in which Sir Pherozeshah's name is mentioned with honour:

"It is now certain that the forthcoming reforms will be of a substantial character and that they will be announced before next Congress meets. For obvious reasons I cannot give you any particulars in this letter, but I know you trust me and will not hesitate to take it from me that our faith in Lord Morley will be fully vindicated in December. What is, however, necessary in order that these reforms should produce their full effect on the public mind in India is that they should be accompanied or immediately followed by important conciliatory action in several directions. And I have strong reasons to believe that the chances of such action being taken largely depend on the manner in which the constitutional party in India rallies round the new Congress and the pronouncements it makes at the next gathering. It is, therefore, of supreme importance that earnest and thoughtful constitutionalists should assemble in large numbers from all parts of the country next Christmas and that the Presidential chair should be occupied by the foremost constitutionalist, Sir P. M. Mehta. The Presidential address of this year will have to practically restate the basis on which our public life is to rest in the immediate future, and the pronouncement is awaited with the utmost interest in influential quarters. Pressure, therefore, must be put on Pherozeshah from all sides so as to overcome his reluctance and the enormous advantage of his presence as President secured to the next Congress. And every possible effort must be made to make the session an eventful one."[7]

It shows one in what great veneration, in what high regard, Gokhale held Pherozeshah. He thought of him as the most befitting President at a crisis in India's affairs, when the old Congress had been practically dissolved and a new Congress on a new basis was to take its place. Lord Minto, intending to conciliate India, announced a scheme of Reforms, in which Gokhale had taken part, and which to him appeared to be fraught with a great deal of benefit to the country.

In 1915 both Gokhale and Sir Pherozeshah departed to the heavenly abode: Gokhale, in the beginning and Pherozeshah at the end of the year. The death of Gokhale naturally created a very great sensation in the country, and at the great public meeting attended by Lord and Lady Willingdon in Bombay to commemorate Gokhale's name and service, when all others had spoken, Sir Pherozeshah was reluctantly called to the platform. He was too much in grief and sorrow to take part in the proceedings. The reporter said that his face had lost its leonine power, his features had fallen, his muscles were drawn, and age infirmities and grief had combined to mark his brow with wrinkles never seen before. When Sir Pherozeshah appeared to take part in the proceedings, he had to make an effort to hold himself and spoke in cheked voice. He made a short speech:

"Even if I attempted to make a long speech, I feel I could not have spoken connectedly and coherently, for the reason that I feel so sad, so depressed, so forsaken, advancing as I am in years, on seeing valued and beloved colleague after colleague dropping away from my side...Telang has been gathered to his fathers, Ranade is no more amongst us, Badrudin has passed away.... Gokhale alas! has now closed his eyes for ever and for ever, and many others whom I could name, are leaving me, one after another, forsaken and desolate. I feel almost alone in the stupendous work for the country which is still pending before us.

"I cannot but recall with a keen sense of regret what plans

Gokhale had laid down, what hopes he had entertained, what work he had chalked out for himself for the development and advancement of the country which he had loved so dearly. Without his help, guidance and co-operation, I do not know how to persevere with the task which we have set before ourselves".[8]

It is true that there were differences between these great men. As a matter of common experience, it is not possible for two great men devoted to the country in the same way and attacking the same problems, with the same equipment of knowledge and patriotism, to agree on every issue. In fact it would be ominous if they did agree. There were differences between them, but they were not so deep to disturb their mutual confidence, or to make one think ill of the other, or to blocking the progress or advancement of the other or mar the good work begun by the other.

The first incident of difference took place in the Bombay Legislative Council when Sir Pherozeshah staged, along with a few friends of his, a walk-out. The Bill was criticized by him and his followers as being very drastic in its character and against the interests of the ryots and peasants of the land. The amendment which he had moved strongly to have the matter postponed, had been voted down by the mechanistic majority of Government. Thus, he walked out along with the three or four others including Chandavarkar. Gokhale too followed, but only after the break. Gokhale, in fact, had protested against the walk out: "This is not becoming of us... we should not do such a thing". But Pherozeshah was very keen. So he wrote to Gokhale that he could not change his resolution. Gokhle ultimately agneed. He said, "Well, I will follow you. I would rather be in the wrong with you than in the right by myself".[9] And when his turn came to take leave of the Council, he did not leave abruptly and in a mood of resentment, as the others had done. He made a speech before he left:

"Your Excellency, May I offer a word of personal explanation? In the remarks which I made this afternoon, I did not like to say anything as to the course I should take if the amendment was lost. I think it my duty, My Lord, now to say that I must follow the course which has been taken by some of my honourable colleagues. I take this course with the greatest reluctance and regret. I mean no disrespect to Your Excellency or to your colleagues personally. It is only an overwhelming sense of duty, which urges me to take this step because I am not prepared to accept even the remotest responsibility of associating myself with this measure which my further presence here would imply."[10]

Gokhale's action did not please Pherozeshah, because he did this after offering a personal explanation to His Excellency and to the Council, which, in Pherozeshah's opinion, they did not deserve.

Here is another letter, not hitherto published. This was written in 1906 and refers to a subject which has been almost forgotten. A Bill was often contemplated, containing different sections in the form of a statute, regarding Reforms in the constitution of the country. Telang had taken great pains in preparing the Bill, but when he consulted Pherozeshah, he put his foot down on it. His instinct in these matters was very sound; he could perceive the conquences of the Bill. Regarding this, Gokhale wrote to V. Krishnaswami Aiyar:

"I start again for England on the 14th April. A serious difficulty has arisen about the draft Bill which I had intended taking with me. Sir P. Mehta has taken a strongly hostile attitude on the subject. He urges that we should not commit ourselves to any definite proposals embodying them in a draft of our own, but that we should ask for as much as we can and throw the responsibility of determining the next installment of reform in the matter on the Government. And in deference to his opinion, which considering his position in public life and his unrivalled experience as Member of Provincial and Supreme Councils, it will not do to ignore, it seems best not to take any draft Bill from here."[11]

This shows what profound respect was paid to Pherozeshah's opinion on these matters, even by those who were so near to him as Gokhale did.

There are three other important matters in which they differed. When Gokhale started the *Servants of India Society* in 1905, he laid the prospectus and his ideas before Pherozeshah. Pherozeshah strongly disapproved of the idea. "I did not know what lines he took; but this Gokhale told me. He told Gokhale that since the lives of the servants of India were to be led on austere lines, since they were to take small allowances from the society, and since they were forbidden to earn anything for themselves or to attend to their personal affairs, Pherozeshah feared that would constitute a sort of superior caste among those, who did not do service to the country in the same way, and that their bearing towards their colleagues and other patriots would be marked perhaps by a feeling of moral superiority. They would hold themselves to be entitled to greater respect from their lay brethren. I mention it, as it is a matter of some importance. You know the kind of people that we are. We do not assume any superior airs. On the other hand, some of you may have noticed that we go about the country almost as if we were marked for an inferior position amongst you."[12]

The next point is the famous Press Act for which Sir S.P. Sinha made himself responsible. Gokhale who was then his colleague, took strong objection to the provisions of the Press Act, introduced many amendments and fought it at every turn. But in the end, though he did not vote for it, he did not vote against it either for the reason that Lord Sinha was the first Executive Councillor to be appointed to assist the Viceroy. Lord Morley had taken great pain and even though he was opposed by all the leading politicians and statesmen in Great Britain, he put them all aside. Unfortunately, Lord Sinha, as soon as he took office, had to introduce this Press Bill, which he hated with all his soul. Its provisions were so restricted, so stringent, and so repressive in character that he declered that he was not going to be responsible for it, and made it clear that he would not pilot it in the Legislative Council. He was willing to resign; though fearful of what might happen in case he resigned and the damping influence it would have on Lord Morley. Many of Sinha's friends gathered round him together with the Chief Justice Sir Lawrence Jenkins in private counsel night and day, and helped him with a great many amendments, which pulled the teeth out of the Bill. Still it was a vicious Bill, and Gokhale, who supported Lord Sinha in all this endeavour behind the scene, told him, "I must take your leave to oppose this Bill at every turn". Sinha said replied: "If you are going to oppose it, allow me to get out of this at once." He threatened to resign and thus pressurised Gokhale not to oppose the Bill. Gokhale, out of deference to him and also out of fear of what might happen in case he did resign, and should this precedent be not appreciated sufficiently in the country, said, "I will go thus far with you. I will speak on the whole in favour of the Bill, but refrain from voting against it, but at the same time in deference to my own conscience, I won't vote for it either!"[13] When this matter came to the ears of Sir Pherozeshah, he was very angry. He said Gokhale had no business to enter into any pact with Sinha. Sinha knew his own business. Why should the representative of the Bombay Presidency go out of his way and stand shoulder to shoulder with Sinha, taking a large part of the odium on himself? He should have voted against it and made his vote known, as having been hostile to that Act. Sir Pherozeshah never forgave Gokhale for this.

Then again, there was the *Elementary Education Bill* in which Gokhale failed to carry Pherozeshah with him for rather administrat' ve reasonns rather than or legislat than with the policy-side of the matter. Sir Pherozeshah did not agree with Gokhale sufficiently in this case.

But the chief point on which they differed was with reference to South Africa. You may remember that in 1914 there was a famous Smuts-Gandhi Pact for the settlement of some of the outstanding points of dispute between the white people and our Indian community. The settlement was reached as it were, with a great act of surrender on our part. Both Gokhale and Gandhi agreed that to save the people (one and a half millions) from the terrible plight into which they had fallen, it was necessary to give up what was then called the right of free immigration of any Indian subject of His Majesty throughout the Empire. This right of immigration was there only in people's assertion and in their claim. It was not there recognised by the Constitution or by the Law. It was expressly denied by all the Dominions. It was, therefore, a kind of right which people asserted, but which on the other side was never allowed. It was, therefore, forced upon the people, and both Gandhi and Gokhale, said to the South African Whites, "We will no longer claim the right of immigrating to this country as often as we like and in such numbers as we like. We will give up the right, and you may pass a law of Immigration, preventing our people from landing on South African shores, if you so like".[14] Pherozeshah did not think that this was a good thing to do. He felt strongly that 'whatever our troubles were we should not have yielded to this.' He felt this so strongly that he did not attend any of the meetings which Gokhale or Gandhi subsequently addressed, describing the state of affairs in South Africa. Nobody at that time could forsee the events that justified Pherozeshah to a great extent. We have withdrawn a great right. This was not due to any weakness on the part of Gokhale or Gandhi, but it is due to the extraordinary notions that the White people in the Dominion had of the Indian community and their right to preserve their civilization from all debasing and degrading association, and furthermore, the economic aspect of maintaining the high standard of life for which they have made great sacrifices.

Two other points need to be mentioned here. One, was the great desire of Gokhale and many others in the country to end the differences that arose at Surat between the moderates and extremists, and that the Congress should again become a large, united all-party Congress. Gokhale was always for reconciliation. His mind did not move on sharp edges. He was a kind, tender-hearted man. He often said: "I want you not to live under the same cloud of dissension, under which most our lives were spent. I wish you to come into an atmosphere of greater cordiality among the people of this country." Though he took great pains over this reconciliation, he did not succeed. Pherozeshah was very angry with him on this: "Let me tell you, we cannot hold them within the Congress and as our friends with a brotherly embrace for a long time. People will come in and start trouble, and then you will have to pass under conditions of far greater difficulty and far greater national sorrow".[15]

The other point was "the attitude that the progressive party in the country should take towards Dr. Besant, who was fast pushing herself in the forefront and threatened to over-reach the Congress and take first place in the political field. Pherozeshah and Wacha and many others looked upon her as the greatest danger. Gokhale, however, had actually joined the Theosophical Society. He was a member, and though he had taken no part whatever in Theosophical consultations and counsel, continued still to be a passive member, and his natural attitude of reverence made him look upon Mrs. Besant as a great figure in the world, remarkable for learning, for world-wide experience, for titanic energy spent in great causes and for untiring service to this country, in education, in religion, and in politics as well." He could not, therefore, bring himself to be in any way antagonistic to Mrs. Besant, "Do not do that. Stand by her." But Wacha and Sir Pherozeshah were absolutely irreconcilable. They never could conquer their suspicion of her, and therefore, to the very end prevented Gokhale and others from having any bargain with her.[16] They also tried to prevent Dadabhai Naoroji from becoming President of the *All-India Home Rule League.* Dadabhai, in a moment of enthusiasm, joined it; though Wacha and Pherozeshah protested against it. Gokhale was different altogether by nature; and therefore, he paid Mrs. Besant personal respect, and made us all pay her a great respect and profound attention.

REFERENCES

1. Sastri, V. S. Srinivasa, *Life and Times of Sir Pherozeshah Mehta, op. cit.*, p. 60.
2. *Ibid.*, p. 61.
3. Sastri, V. S. Srinivasa, *My Master Gokhale*, Madras: Model Publications, 1946.
4. *Ibid.*, p. 248.
5. *Speeches of Gokhale*, Madras: Model Publications, Vol. II, 1920, p. 178.
6. *Ibid.*, pp. 237-38.
7. *Gokhale Papers*, Madras: Servants of India Society, n.d. pp. 242-43.
8. *Ibid.*, p. 482.
9. Sastri, V. S. Srinivasa, *Life and Times of Sir Pherozeshah Mehta, op. cit.*, p. 69.
10. *Gokhale Speeches*, Vol. I, p. 444.
11. Sastri, V. S. Srinivasa, *My Master Gokhale op. cit.*, p. 256.
12. Sastri, V. S. Srinivasa, *Life and Times of Sir Pherozeshah Mehta, op. cit.*, p. 70.
13. *Ibid.*, p. 71.
14. *Ibid.*, p. 73.
15. *Ibid.*
16. *Ibid.*

6

MEHTA AND CONGRESS

The activities of Indian reformers in the last quarter of Nineteenth Century found their most practical expression in the establishment of an organization, which for more than thirty years has laboured with a success, which its promoters could hardly have dreamt of, to rouse the political consciousness of the people, and to direct and foster the national movement. The Indian National Congress came into being towards the close of 1885, timidly and unobtrusively, but under circumstances which were full of promise for the future.

It was in the time of Lord Lytton that the conviction began to gather ground that sóme action was needed to counteract the growing forces of reaction, which were threatening the peaceful progress and development of the country. The Vernacular Press Act had greatly agitated the Indian mind; all over the country sober leaders of thought had since been exchanging views on the situation that had arisen, and laying plans for the future. There was a unanimity of feeling that India could no longer afford to stand and gaze, and that the time had arrived for the organization of a popular movement, which would arrest the reactionary tendencies increasingly manifested in the policy of Government and rouse the people to a sense of their wrongs.

With the arrival of Lord Ripon, a considerable improvement in the situation took place, and for some time nothing was done. It was not till 1883 that the first step was taken by Allan Octavian Hume—whose distinguished career in the Civil Service had just come to an end—in a circular letter, dated 1 March, 1883, addressed to the graduates of the Calcutta University. It was a stirring appeal to the young men to Bengal to band themselves into a body of earnest workers for the national cause. If only fifty people came forward in the first instance, an organization could be started, which would develop into a national movement in course of time. It may be mentioned in passing, that the lines suggested by Hume were more or less adopted by Gokhale nearly three decades later in his Servants of India Society. The appeal was coupled with a stern warning of the consequences of a lukewarm patriotism:

"If you, the picked men, the most highly educated of the nation, cannot, scorning personal ease and selfish objects, make a resolute struggle to secure greater freedom for yourselves and your country, a more impartial administration, a larger share in the administration of your own affairs, then we your friends are wrong and your adversaries right, then are Lord Ripons' noble aspirations for your good fruitless and visionary, then, at present at any rate, all hopes of progress are at an end, and India truly neither lacks nor deserves any better government than she enjoys."[1]

The result of this stirring manifesto was the formation of the Indian National Union towards the end of 1884, which, in consultation with the Bombay Presidency Association, the Sarvajanik Sabha and other political organizations, arranged to hold an All-India Conference in December 1885, for the purpose of deciding upon a plan of political campaign, and effecting a closer co-operation between the leaders of thought in various parts of the country. Hume's original idea was to discuss social matters only, as he thought that, the recognised public bodies which were doing political work in various centres would suffer in importance. But this view had to be abandoned at an early stage. It was hoped that the Conference would form the germ of an Indian Parliament, which, properly constituted and conducted, would be an effective reply to the assertion that India was unfit for any form of representative institutions. Previous to this, the three leading Associations of Calcutta had partly carried out the object in view, and had got together a number of people from different provinces for exchange of views, and for settling a common programme of action.

The honour of holding the Conference was accorded to Poona, and the *Sarvajanik Sabha* undertook to make all the necessary arrangements at its own cost, constituting itself for the occasion as a sort of Reception Committee. The place selected was the palace of the Peshwas at the foot of the Parvati Hill. Before the preliminaries were settled, Hume, who was the life and soul of the movement, went and saw Lord Dufferin and placed before him his ideas of national regeneration. The Viceroy showed himself friendly, sympathetic, and it was at his instance that Hume, who had social reform in the forefront of his programme, decided in consultation with his friends to give the proposed organization a political character. Lord Dufferin had pointed out the difficulty experienced by Government in ascertaining the real wants and wishes of the people, and had expressed his conviction that it would be advantageous to have some responsible body through which the best Indian opinion could be gathered. An omniscient bureaucracy had apparently, not then laid claim to an exclusive acquaintance the wants and feelings of the masses, nor, it seems, had thought of the mischievous consequences of subordinating social to political reform! All this was left to latter-day critics, after the Congress began to be troublesome and ceased to bask in the shine of official favour.

The policy of the Conference having been laid down, Hume proceeded to England to try and secure the movement against representation and calumny. He saw many prominent men, Lord Ripon, Lord Loreburn (then Mr. Robert Reid) and a large number of members of the House of Commons. He received assurances and sympathy from them, as well as from a section of the Liberal Press, which promised to publish messages sent through agency of the Indian Telegraph Union, which had mischievous activities of Reuter. When everything was satisfactorily settled, Hume returned to India in October and found Poona preparing for the great occasion. But it was destined that the historic capital of the Deccan should not have the honour of holding first Congress in her midst. An outbreak of cholera occurred, and at the eleventh hour the venue had to be changed. Bombay at once came to the rescue, and promptly made the necessary arrangements. The trustees of the Goculdas Tejpal Boarding School at Gowalia Tank, of whom Telang was one, placed the spacious building at the disposal of the organizers. By the 27th December, everything was ready for the reception of the 'representatives,' as they were called. The whole of the day, and part of the night too, was spent in mutual introductions and informal discussions. In the evening, a large number of prominent citizens came to welcome the representatives, and to express appreciation of the task to which they had set their hands.

On the fateful morning of 28 December, 1885, seventy-two good men representing a cross-section of the most advanced political opinion, sat down to chalk out a programme of action. It was a happy circumstance that Bombay should have been ultimately chosen as the meeting place of the first Congress. It was in Bombay that the foundations of Local Self-Government had been laid, and it was appropriate that Bombay should also be the birthplace of the national movement. The honour of presiding on the occasion went to W.C. Bonnerji one of the most eminent leaders Bengal has produced. At first, the idea was to ask the Governor of Bombay, Lord Reay, a statesman of liberal ideas, who belonged to the famous group of "Philosophical Radicals," to take the chair, but the matter being referred to Lord Dufferin, he deprecated the suggestion on the ground that it would be undesirable, from more points of view than one, for the head of the province actively to associate himself with what should essentially be a popular movement.[2]

The gathering was small, being confined to the delegates mentioned, and a few visitors, among whom were Sir William Wedderburn, Mr. Justice Jardine, Professor Wordsworth, Colonel Phelps, Ramkrishna Bhandarkar, and M.G. Ranade, then: a judge of the Small Causes Court at Poona. But it was a representative gathering, which included leaders of thought in all parts of the country. In the words of the President, "never had so important and comprehensive an assemblage occurred within historical times on the soil of India." Some there were, advanced in years, like the Grand Old Man of India; others like Bonnerji, Telang, Subramaniya Iyer, Wacha and Pherozeshah, still young and enthusiastic, and full of hopes for the future. All alike were greatly in earnest and fired with a noble purpose. Year after year, these early stalwarts stood on the Congress platform, unmindful of ridicule and obloquy, and with their faith unimpaired in the justice of their cause, and in its ultimate triumph. Their faith was large in time, and many of them lived to see the dawn of a brighter day.[3]

The proceedings commenced with the election of the President, moved by Hume and seconded and supported by Messers. Subramania Iyer and Telang. Bonnerji in acknowledging honour done to him, made a short speech—the portentous orations of later days were then unknown—in which he explained objects of the movement referring to the authority of those who had gathered there to speak on behalf of their countrymen, he said he did not claim that they were representatives of the people in the same sense in which the members of the House of Commons were representatives of the constituencies, "but if community of sentiments, community of feelings and community of wants enabled anyone to speak on behalf of others, then assuredly they might justly claim to be the representatives of the people of India."[4] At the end of the speech, Mr. Bonnerji affirmed the loyalty of the Congress to the British connection. Nine resolutions were moved which, among other things, demanded a Royal Commission of inquiry into the working of the Indian administration, the abolition of the Indian Council, the expansion of the Legislative Councils, the curtailment of military expenditure and the institution of simultaneous examinations for the Civil Service. Most of these resolutions have become hardy annuals, and need not be noticed here, but it is interesting to note that, in the resolution dealing with the expansion of Legislative Councils, the suggestion was made "that a Standing Committee of the House of Commons should be constituted to receive and consider any formal protests that may be recorded majorities of such Councils against the exercise by the Executive power, which would be vested in it, of overruling the decision of such majorities."[5]

Pherozeshah's share in the proceedings of this historic Congress was not inconsiderable. He was entrusted with the seconding of the first proposition, moved by G. Subramania Iyer, which approved of the promised committee of inquiry into the working of the Indian administration. Speaking on the resolution, Pherozeshah contended that the body charged with the inquiry should be so constituted that it could be in a position to pursue its investigations in this country itself, taking evidence here, and that Indians should be represented on it. He was of opinion that if the inquiry was not granted in the manner pointed out, it would be almost better to have no inquiry at all. Parliamentary Committees and Royal Commissions were not to be had at short intervals, and it would be disastrous to have a body composed mainly of Englishmen sitting in judgement upon themselves. The conclusions at which such a body would arrive would be superficially plausible, but essentially unsound. They would be accepted as guiding principles for at least another twenty years and the mischief thus ensuing would be incalculable. These observations seem to have suggested the amendment, which was moved by Daya Narain Jethmal, a representative of Sind, which recommended that the inquiry should be entrusted to a Royal Commission on which the people of India should be represented, and which should take evidence both in England and in India. The amendment was accepted by Pherozeshah, and after an interesting discussion, in which Messrs. Hume, Wacha, Telang, Malabari and Dadabhai Naoroji took part, it was carried unanimously.

Another proposal with which Pherozeshah identified himself was in connection with the annexation of Upper Burma. He asked for leave to introduce the subject, as it did not find a place on the agenda. He said he did not wish to go into the question of the annexation which he considered unwise, unjust and immoral. He only desired to look at the matter from the Indian point of view, and viewing it so, he was of opinion that Burma should be made a Crown Colony, as otherwise, he was afraid she would prove a drag on Indian progress. Lord Dufferin had said that the weakness of the North-West Frontier disabled him from giving as much attention as he liked to home affairs, and Pherozeshah did not want that the North-East Frontier should be added to the list of the Viceroy's distractions. With Ceylon in the South, and Burma in the North-East as Crown Colonies, the speaker thought they could ask with greater strength and reason for more liberal institutions in India than she possessed. These remarks were greeted with so much applause that the President said that he would take that as equivalent to a grant of leave to introduce the motion. Pherozeshah accordingly moved:

That this Congress deprecates the annexation of Upper Burma, and considers that if the Government unfortunately decide on annexation, the entire country of Burma should be separated from the Indian Viceroyalty, and constituted a Crown Colony, as distinct in all matters from the government of this country Ceylon.[6]

After some discussion, the proposition was carried. At the present moment, while Indian politicians are crying aloud that Burma should be regarded as an integral part of India, the bureaucracy is jealously seeking to guard the province from contamination with the currents of Indian political life. Such are the changes which *whirligig of time* brings about.

The resolution on Burma practically finished the business of the session. At the close, resounding cheers were given for the Queen Empress and for Hume, to whose energy, driving force and burning love for the land in which he had spent the best years of his life, were due in a great measure the inception and success of the first National Congress of the people of India. Small as it was in numbers, it might be regarded as voicing the opinions of a number of politically minded Indians. The resolutions which were carried at its session were generally adopted at meetings held all over the country.

The proceedings of the Congress evoked widespread interest, and were noticed at some length in *The Times,* whose Bombay correspondent wrote a sympathetic account of the movement. Commenting upon it, the 'Thunderer' could not resist the temptation of indulging in sentiments which are the usual stock-in-trade of the die-hard. After referring to the manner in which Bombay had substantiated her claim to be the first city in India by being the gathering place of the first national assembly, it went on to give a qualified approval to some of the resolutions and an unqualified disapproval to others. After detailing the latter, the journal remarked:

The first question which this series of resolutions will suggest is whether India is ripe for the transformation which they involve. If this can be answered in the affirmative, the days of English rule are numbered. If India can govern itself, our stay in the country is no longer called for. All we have to do is to preside over the construction of the new system and then leave it to work. The lawyers and schoolmasters and newspaper editors will step into the vacant place and will conduct affairs with no help from us. Those who know India best will be the first to recognize the absurd impracticability of such a change. The educated classes may find fault with their exclusion from full political rights. Political privileges they can obtain in the degree in which they prove themselves deserving of them. But it was by force that India was won, and it is by force that India must be governed, in whatever hands the government of the country may be vested. If we were to withdraw, it would be in favour not of the most fluent tongue, or of the most ready pen, but the strongest arm and the sharpest sword.[7]

When the Congress met at Allahabad in 1888, it did so in an atmosphere of bitterness and strife. The Reception Committee had great difficulty in finding a site, and it was only when a private mansion with extensive grounds was secured through the patriotic efforts of a certain nobleman, that the Congress was able to overcome the obstructions placed in its way. But this was not all. An anti-Congress propaganda had been started, led, unfortunately, by that distinguished Mohammedan, Sir Syed Ahmed, and supported chiefly, as Eardley Norton put it, by an "array of illiterate knights and *rajahs*, who atone for their defective education by the violence of their expletives."[8]

Authoritative official condemnation was not wanting, either. In a famous speech at the St. Andrew's dinner at Calcutta on 30th December, 1888, Lord Dufferin, who was in a sense the originator of the Congress movement, denounced its ideals and methods in language which has often been quoted. "Some intelligent, loyal, patriotic and well-meaning men," said he, "are desirous of taking, I will not say a further step in advance, but a very big jump into the unknown, by the application to India of democratic methods of government, and the adoption of a parliamentary system which England herself has reached by slow degrees, and through the discipline of many centuries." His Lordship ended by characterizing the educated classes as a "microscopic minority," and their demand for representative institutions as eminently unconstitutional.

Equally famous as this viceregal criticism was the correspondence which passed in October 1888, between Hume and Sir Auckland Colvin, the Lieutenant-Governor of what were then known as the North-Western Provinces. Hume wrote to Sir

Auckland, telling him that he was generally regarded as hostile to the Congress and as the inspirer of all the organized attacks upon it, and asking him for an open expression of his views. The letters which passed between them were a striking exposition of the points of view of the two antagonists, and when published found a wide circle of readers.

Such was the atmosphere in which the Congress held its fourth sessions at Allahabad during the Christmas of 1888, under the presidentship of George Yule, one of the leading members of the English community in Calcutta. Not "disappointed civilian" was he, nor a glib-tongued lawyer, but a prosperous merchant with no grievances to air, nor prejudices against his caste. The selection of the chairman of the Reception Committee was equally happy. Pandit Ajodhyanath was one of the foremost men in the province, with a character which stood as high as his professional and public reputation.

As may be expected from the opposition encountered by the Congress, the proceedings were of a more than usually lively character. The presence of Raja Shivaprasad—a henchman of Sir Auckland Colvin—who had got himself elected as a delegate with the object of introducing discord within the ranks, threatened at one time to create serious disorder, but the leading spirits of the Congress defeated the attempt, and the obnoxious Raja was quietly escorted home. The presidential address was a weighty and dignified pronouncement. A strong note of optimism and faith in the future ran through the utterance:

"All movements of the kind in which we are concerned pass through several phases as they run their course. The first is one of ridicule. That is followed, as the movement progresses, by one of abuse, which is usually succeeded by partial concession and misapprehension of aim, accompanied by warnings against taking 'big jumps into the unknown'. The final stage of all is a substantial adoption, of the object of the movement with some expression of surprise that it was not adopted before."[9]

Pherozeshah's contribution to the deliberations was confined to two or three subjects. He moved the proposition for the appointment of the President in a few felicitous phrases. He spoke with effect on the resolutions dealing with the public service question to which he had given much thought and study. In January 1888, he had been invited to give evidence before the Public Service Commission, which had been appointed after the failure of the Statutory Service had been recognized on all hands. Both in his written and oral evidence, Pherozeshah had taken up a strong attitude. He had condemned the various expedients suggested for the improvement of the Statutory Service, and had pressed for a fair and open competition under equal conditions. Failing simultaneous examinations, he had favoured the foundation of numerous scholarships, "tenable by natives in England for the purpose of enabling them to qualify and to compete for the Covenanted Civil Service, provided these scholarships were not bestowed by any system of nomination of any kind or sort whatever, but by free and open competition in India."[10]

The conclusions which the Commission had arrived at were discussed with much knowledge and ability at the Allahabad Congress. While it was conceded that an advance had been made, dissatisfaction was expressed at the manner in which the question of simultaneous examinations had been dealt with. The resolution on the subject was proposed by Eardley Norton, one of the earliest and warmest supporters of the Congress, with a reputation for ability and independence which stood very high. It expressed appreciation of the concessions proposed by the Commission, but emphatically declared that full justice would never be done to the people of the country until the Civil Service examination was held simultaneously in England and in India.

Pherozeshah seconded the proposition and put the case for the larger employment of the people of the country on the ground of political as well as economic necessity. Dadabhai Naoroji had over and over again pointed out that apart from every other consideration, it was sound economy to associate Indians more closely in the administration of the country. Pherozeshah, going further, contended that the political necessity was even greater than the economic. According to him:

"When the time came to settle the principles on which British rule in India was to be carried on, it was clearly recognized by those sober statesmen who guided the destinies of England at that time, that even for Orientals an absolute despotism was an impossible creed in practical politics. It was clearly recognized that even the most benevolent and most paternal despotism must, if it wants to be stable and permanent, place its roots in the country in which it carries on that rule; and this principle was soberly though eloquently enunciated by Lord Macaulay in 1833, when he said that for the sake of English honour and English wisdom, it was absolutely imperative that the natives of this country should have an equal share in the administration."[11]

The venue of 1889 Session of Congress was Bombay. The venue was decided upon after a consideration of the relative merits of Poona and Bombay. At first, it appears from a letter of Ranade to Pherozeshah written in the early part of January, the once proud capital of the Peshwas was not anxious to enjoy the honour of which she had on a former occasion been deprived by a cruel chance. But later on, her young men bestirred themselves, and she was eager to shoulder the burden of holding the Congress in her midst. Ultimately, however, Bombay once again robbed her of the privilege.

From the personality of those who took a leading part in it, and the numbers that consequently flocked to it, the Bombay session proved to be the most memorable gathering of the "unconventional convention" that had yet taken place. Very few Congresses indeed have surpassed it in brilliance. The presidential chair was occupied by Sir William Wedderburn, who had retired from service two years previously, loved and honoured by all who had come in contact with him. The glowing tributes that were paid to his worth on his retirement from office, by the leaders of public opinion in Bombay, at a Town Hall meeting convened by the Sheriff, were no conventional expressions of regard, but were the outcome of a genuine appreciation of Sir William's rare devotion to the country; and that feeling found further expression in the people offering him on the present occasion the highest honour that lay within their gift.[12]

The privilege of welcoming the delegates to this historic Congress was conceded to Pherozeshah as an appropriate recognition of the fact of his being the most outstanding figure in the public life of Western India at this period. A more popular selection could not have been made, at least, from the point of view of a Bombay audience. But the biggest 'draw' of all was the presence of that great champion of democracy, Charles Bradlaugh, whose magnetic eloquence had thrilled vast audiences in his native land, and whose stormy career had deeply struck the public imagination. He had been persuaded to take an interest in Indian questions by the friends of this country in England, and had addressed a number of public meetings. He had recently prepared a draft Bill for introduction into Parliament for the reform of the Legislative Councils. It embodied in legal form what was then believed to be the general view of the Congress on the subject. Mr. Bradlaugh's object in visiting India was to ascertain on the spot the mature views of the educated classes on certain important points in connection with the Bill, which had been translated into many Indian languages, and had received most careful consideration all over the country.

It was a great gathering. The number of delegates was 1,889, corresponding curiously with the year in which the session was held. A vast structure had been erected on a site at Byculla belonging to Sir Albert Sassoon and next to his mansion, the "Sans-Souci," to accommodate the delegates and visitors, who numbered nearly 6,000. The burden of making the necessary arrangements fell mostly upon the Chairman of the Reception Committee, and on the local secretary, the indefatigable Dinshaw Wacha, whose untiring efforts to promote the success of the Bombay session were afterwards appreciated by the presentation of a piece of plate by the Reception Committee.[13]

It was a worthy occasion for the exercise of Pherozeshah's oratorical gifts, and he rose splendidly to it. Sarcasm, banter, ridicule were among the weapons with which he usually confounded his opponents, and he employed them with deadly effect in his speech of welcome to the delegates of the Congress. It was a telling vindication of the essential loyalty and national character of the movement. At the outset, the Chairman contended that, though the delegates present might not be the chosen of the people by any scientific mode of election, they virtually and substantially represented them, their wants, wishes, sentiments and aspirations in all the various ways in which representation manifests and works itself out in the early stages of its progressive development. He went on to recount the services which the Congress had directly and indirectly done to the country. It had brought into clear and emphatic recognition the fact of the growth of the national idea amongst the people. It had done that which was a necessary prelude to all reform, a thorough sifting and searching of some of the most vital of Indian political problems.

And now that the proposals of the Congress have bravely stood the test, our opponents have recourse to the familiar device, which is so often employed to cover retreat, and they are lost in wonder that we are making so much fuss about things which have nothing new in them, and which have been long contemplated by many an Anglo-Indian statesman at the head of affairs. Now, gentlemen, we are quite ready at once to plead guilty to this not very dreadful impeachment. But though it may not be said of these statesmen, what was once said of the anti-Reform party in England, and can certainly be said of some Anglo-Indians, that they never have anything kind or generous to say of the Indian people, this may surely be said of them, that though they do sometimes have something generous to say of the Indians, they have never shown the slightest disposition to confer upon them any portion of political rights. If the Congress has done nothing more than quicken into action these political *Yogis*, so long lost in contemplation, it will not have laboured in vain.

When the cheers which greeted this sentiment had subsided, Pherozeshah passed on to deal with the opposition to the Congress, which by a lot of wire-pulling had culminated in the formation of an Anti-Congress United Patriotic Association. He referred to the activities of the two leading spirits of the organization, and drew a humorous picture of the difficulties which had arisen through the combination of two such personalities:

They were like the Scotch terrier who was so covered with hair, that you could not tell which was the head or which was the tail of it. Sir Syed Ahmed pulled vigorously one way, Raja Shiva Prasad as vigorously the other; and they so pulled between them the poor popinjay they had set up, that it burst, and poured out—to the amazement of a few and the amusement of us all—not the real patriotic stuff with which it had been announced to be filled, but the whitest and purest sawdust.

Referring next to the charge of disloyalty, Pherozeshah maintained that in its keen solicitude for the safety and permanence of the Empire, in which lay implanted the roots of the welfare, the prosperity and good government of the country, the Congress was more loyal than Anglo-Indians themselves. He concluded his address by paying a graceful tribute to Bradlaugh and offering a hearty welcome to him on behalf of the Congress.[14]

The speech was well received. "The whole assembly laughed and cheered and clapped their hands with an excited delight, which showed how they echoed the sentiments expressed by the speaker." Such demonstrations by themselves, perhaps, do not mean much. No superlative effort is required to rouse an audience charged with emotion; various circumstances lend adventitious aid. But the speech earned the appreciation of a wider public, and the papers next morning spoke of it as an eloquent and vigorous pronouncement. There was criticism, of course, of the point of view of the speaker, and of the distinguished President who followed him. One journal, by no means unsympathetic towards Indian national aspirations, remarked:

Mr. Pherozeshah Mehta yesterday spoke very confidently of the national spirit whose growth had been fostered by the Congress, and Sir William Wedderburn described the aims of the movement to revive the national spirit of the country. It was fortunate for both gentlemen that there was no *advocatus diaboli* at hand to ask them to define the meaning of the word. There never was a time when the term national had any other than a local meaning in India.[15]

From the chairmanship of the Reception Committee to the presidentship of the Congress, is a natural transition, and in Pherozeshah's case it took place rapidly. The very next year after the Bombay Congress, he found himself installed in the presidential chair in Calcutta, an honour than which there was then no higher to which a worker in the national cause could aspire. It was said by unfriendly critics that the honour was going a-begging, and that it was offered to Herbert Gladstone and several others before it fell to the lot of Pherozeshah. However that may be, there is no doubt that the latter richly deserved the distinction which his countrymen conferred upon him. Though still in the prime of life, he had a record behind him of which older leaders might well have been proud. Despite the worries and distractions of a busy practice, he had been able to associate himself with public movements touching the corporate life of the people at many points, and had his mark in everyone of them. It was, therefore, in the fitness of things, that the politically-minded classes in all provinces should call upon him to guide their deliberations in the parliament which they had set up.

The election gave universal satisfaction. Public opinion was reflected in the Press, and many newspapers contained appreciatory references to the President-elect. The comments of *The Gujarati* may be singled out as giving the best presentation of the popular view of Pherozeshah's personality:

"A better selection it would have been impossible to make, and we must heartily congratulate him upon the great honour bestowed upon him in recognition of the exceptionally independent attitude he has always taken in public life, and of his long and zealous public services. Gifted with great oratorical powers, endowed with a generous heart and highly trained intellect, possessed of a commanding voice and presence that enforces willing obedience, and eminently fitted by nature to be a leader of men, Mr. Mehta is bound to leave upon the assembled delegates and visitors an impression that it would be difficult to efface.[16]

Year after year the cry of the Congress went unheeded, its ponderous resolutions were contemptuously looked upon as the demands of noisy agitators or impatient idealists. The new party would, therefore, have nothing to do with the 'policy of mendicancy' of the Congress and its veteran leaders. The Deccan and Bengal were the two principal centres of the new gospel that was preached from the Press and platform by an ever-increasing band of youthful and aggressive politicians under the inspiration of men like Messrs. Bepin Chandra Pal, Aurobindo Ghosh, and that stormy petrel of Indian politics, Bal Gangadhar Tilak.

The first manifestations of the new spirit, so far as it affected the national movement embodied in the Congress, were evidenced at Benares in 1905, when Gokhale was in the chair. Anticipating trouble, he had wired to Chimanlal Setalvad, insisting upon Pherozeshah's presence at the session as without him there was a real danger of the Congress being committed to wild and impossible positions. Gokhale felt convinced that the proceedings would end harmoniously, and Pherozeshah's lead followed by an overwhelming majority if he was personally present. No serious injury was done to the Congress cause, however, in spite of Pherozeshah keeping away though it was felt by many that his presence would have completely frustrated the partly successful attempts which the new party had made to drag the Congress at its heels.

In the following year at Calcutta, the breach widened, and the differences between the two wings of the Congress became more acute. An open rupture was only prevented by the action of Pherozeshah, Gokhale and one or two other Moderate leaders in installing the Grand Old Man of India in the presidential chair. It was a happy inspiration. The presence of the venerable apostle of Indian nationalism, long past the patriarchal age, coming from a far-off land to render his last service to the people whom he loved so well, exercised a restraining influence on the noisiest Extremist, and prevented a definite split within the ranks. Even so, the bark of the Congress was driven to perilous waters, and violent storms threatened to engulf it.

Immediately the Calcutta session was over, the apostles of the new cult started vigorous propaganda work throughout the country. Tilak opened the campaign at Allahabad in January 1907, and he was shortly followed by his lieutenant Khaparde at Nagpur, where the ensuing Congress was to be held. The Moderate leaders were freely vilified by nationalist scribblers and orators, and were described as the most debased of humankind. The work of preparation for the Congress at Nagpur was marked by the most disgraceful intrigues and scenes that ever disfigured the political annals of the country.

Finding that Nagpur was determined upon wrecking the Congress, Pherozeshah and his party reluctantly felt compelled to change the venue to some other place. At a meeting of the All-India Congress Committee held at his house, it was decided to transfer the sittings to Surat, which had gallantly come forward to undertake the heavy responsibility of holding the Congress in its midst. The rage of the Extremists knew no bounds. Their newspapers and politicians showered unstinted abuse on the Moderate leaders, particularly Pherozeshah, who was regarded as primarily responsible for the change of venue and whose inflexible will and masterful personality they recognized as the greatest obstacle to the success of their manoeuvres. Surat was jeered at as a sleepy hollow, and all sorts of threats were held out to those responsible for the arrangements for the forthcoming session.

It is true that differences of outlook and methods between the two parties made an early rupture inevitable. The Extremists had charted the seas and mapped out the course they were determined to pursue. The Moderates were equally determined to go along the path they had trodden with a dogged perseverance for many a year. At their head, supported by Gokhale and a band of able and loyal adherents, stood Pherozeshah, with his great skill in the handling of men and his unbending will in matters of principle. Such a dreaded opponent could neither be converted nor crushed. Small hope, therefore, that the two parties could have evolved a common programme or stood for long on a common platform. But the fight at Surat was not the natural outcome of a clash of principles. It was a piece of organized hooliganism, bringing a measure of discredit upon the national movement which clung to it for years. It also infused a bitterness into the political life of India, which had a baleful effect on the future course of events.[17]

When the Extremists contemplated their handiwork on the morrow of that eventful session, it was to be overwhelmed with a feeling that a cardinal blunder had been committed. In the euphemistic language of Khaparde, "regret at the occurrences, irrespective of the causes that led to them, appeared to be universal, coupled with a desire that a modus operandi should be found to bring all concerned together and arrange for an adjustment, honourable to all alike and calculated to further the cause of the Congress." The Nationalist Party clearly saw that in wrecking the Congress, it had lost a powerful weapon for the furtherance of its political purposes, and it was anxious to repair the tactical mistake it had committed.

It carried on a vigorous campaign in favour of a united Congress and strove hard to show that the differences between the two parties were not irreconcilable.

It was at this moment, when a mood of doubt and hesitancy was seizing even the sober and the thoughtful, that Bhupendranath Basu wrote to Pherozeshah asking for an exprcssion of his views on the proposed re-union of the parties. The reply was in the nature of a bomb-shell thrown in the camp of the Extremists. Said he:

"I cannot help saying that there is a great deal of mawkish sentimentality in the passionate appeals for union at all cost. For my part, I think it is most desirable that each set of distinct convictions should have its separate Congress. To jumble them up in one body confuses the real understanding of the extent to which opinion really tends in one direction or another, and it is not possible to make out what the dimensions of the cleavage and difference of opinion existing on any particular question are.

"It is, therefore, desirable that persons holding nearly the same opinions and principles should organize themselves into bodies where they can expound them and lay them before the public in a clear and consistent form. The public could then have the issue clearly before them, and their deliberate judgement can declare itself by the growing favour they would accord to any particular association.

"For God's sake let us have done with all inane and slobbery whine about unity where there is really none. Let each consistent body of views and principles have its own Congress in an honest and straightforward way, and let God, i.e., truth and wisdom, judge between us all."[18]

The letter, widely published, was the topic of the hour everywhere. Sober politicians throughout the country admired its manly tone and its strong commonsense. In equal measure, it received the condemnation of Extremist politicians, who were furious at what was undoubtedly a knockout blow calculated to put an end to their little campaign, 'Choice epithets of cultured Billingsgate' was the comment of one of their organs on the offending letter.

It is necessary at this point to anticipate matters a little and to follow the fortunes of the Congress somewhat further on its onward journey. The Madras session, which followed the Surat split, had proved a success and falsified the gloomy forebodings of hostile critics. The struggle was not at an end, however, and there were many in the camp of the Moderates who were anxious to close up the ranks and sighed for a united Congress.

The next session was to be held at Lahore, and it was expected that a concerted opposition would be offered to the newly framed constitution. A strong president was required in the circumstances, and the choice of the Provincial Congress Committees almost unanimously fell on Pherozeshah. The only dissentient voice was that of Bengal which, more than any other province, desired a rapprochement and which did not relish the idea of having at the helm a resolute man who knew his own mind and had his own way of dealing with timidity and vacillation.

Matters were in this state when one fine morning, just a fortnight before the due date, the country was startled by the news that Pherozeshah had suddenly resigned the Presidentship of the Congress. The telegram, which conveyed the decision to Lala Harkishan Lal, Chairman of the Reception Committee, was as brief as it was enigmatic:

"I deeply regret that owing to a combination of unexpected circumstances, I am compelled to relinquish the honour."[19]

The country was bewildered. Not even the closest friends of Pherozeshah suspected his intentions or could guess at the reasons prompting this extraordinary step which threw the Congress into utter confusion. The President-elect was as silent and mysterious as the Sphinx. The air became thick with rumours and surmises. Some said that Pherozeshah had lost faith in his former political followers and associates, and did not care again to run the risk of insult and molestation. Others concluded that 'the deep political reasons supposed to underlie his action had no better foundation than a meticulous reluctance to preside over a Congress that bade fair to be either a frost or a riot'. Yet others declared that while Pherozeshah was well aware of the strong feeling against him in certain circles, he accepted the presidentship in the anticipation that the opposition would gradually evaporate in face of the settled fact. Finding that this was not the case, and that in fact only a very few days before criticism had been strongly expressed, with characteristic impulsiveness he had suddenly decided to resign rather than occupy a position, his fitness for which was not acquiesced in by all parties.

A stout and fearless fighter, the act was strangely inconsistent with the whole record of his life. From the day he had stood up bravely, while a very young man, in defence of the Crawford regime, against a host of hostile critics, he had never paltered with his convictions, or run away from a fight because the odds were against him, and it is hardly possible that on the present occasion he shrank from fear. But whatever the motives operating on his mind, it cannot be gainsaid that his decision was as unwise as it was unfortunate. There was trouble and unrest in the land, a wave of discontent was sweeping over the country, anarchism had reared its ugly head, its bloody trail was steadily lengthening. The voice of reason and moderation had been silenced. In the counsels of Government, reactionary influences were at work, and repression was rampant, growing with the growth of the new forces that had arisen. Not even the Reforms seemed able to stem the tide of sedition and anarchy and the repressive legislation they brought in their train.

At such a moment, it is easy to understand how anxiously India was waiting for a lead, for some weighty pronouncement on the attitude, both of the Government and the people. But the lead was never given, and the man best fitted to sound the note of reason and true statesmanship, and to inspire the country with his own robust optimism and his abiding faith in peaceful and ordered progress, had retreated, with an abrupt gesture, into the background and left his following wondering and helpless.

REFERENCES

1. Mody, Homi, *Sir Pherozeshah Mehta, op. cit.*, p. 101.
2. Zaidi, A.M. et al., *The Encycolpaedia of Indian National Congress*, New Delhi: S. Chand & Co., 1980, p. 10.
3. *Ibid.*
4. *Ibid.*, p. 69.

5. *Ibid.*
6. Mody, Homi, *Sir Pherozeshah Mehta, op. cit.*, p. 106.
7. *Ibid.*, pp. 106-107.
8. Zaidi, A.M. et al., *The Encycolpaedia of Indian National Congress, op. cit.*, p. 170.
9. Mody, Homi, *Sir Pherozeshah Mehta, op. cit.*, p. 131.
10. *Ibid.*
11. *Ibid.*, p. 132.
12. Zaidi, A.M. et al., *The Encycolpaedia of Indian National Congress, op. cit.*, pp. 422-37.
13. *Ibid.*
14. *Ibid.*
15. *Ibid.*
16. *Ibid.*, p. 564.
17. *Ibid.*, Vol. 5, p. 177.
18. *Ibid.*, pp. 220-27.
19. *Ibid.*, pp. 470-75.

BIBLIOGRAPHY

Ambirajan, S., *Political Economy and Monetary Management in India, 1766-1914* (Madras: Affiliated East West Press), 1984.

Athalye, D.V., *The Life of Lokmanya Tilak* (Poona: Annasahib Chiploonkar), 1921.

Azad, A.K., *India Wins Freedom* (New York: Longman), 1960.

Banerjea, S.N., *A Nation in Making: Being the Reminiscence of Fifty Years* (London: Milford), 1925.

Banerji, A.K. *Aspects of Indo-British Economic Relations, 1858-1898* (Bombay: Oxford University Press), 1982.

Banerji, Arun, *Finances in the Early Raj: Investments and the External Sector* (New Delhi: Sage Publications), 1995.

Black, R.D. *Collison, Economic Thought and the Irish Question, 1817-1870* (Cambridge: Cambridge University Press), 1960.

Bapat, S.V. (ed.), *Gleanings from Tilak's Writings and Speeches* (Poona: S.V. Bapat), 1926.

Bapat, S.V. (ed.) *The Reminiscences and the Anecdotes of Lokmanya Tilak*, Vol. II (Poona: S. V. Bapat), 1925.

Blaug, Mark, "Kuhn *versus* Lakatos or Paradigms *versus* Research Programmes in the history of economics" in *Method and Appraisal in Economics*, edited by Spiro J. Latsis (Cambridge: Cambridge University Press), 1976.

Blaug, Mark, *Economic Theory in Retrospect* (Cambridge: Cambridge University Press), 1978.

Bose, S.C., *The Indian Struggle (1920-34),* (Calcutta: Publications for Netaji Publishing Society), 1948.

Cashman, Richard I., *The Myth of Lokmanya* (Berkeley: University of California Press), 1975.

Central Statistical Organisation, *National Accounts Statistics: Sources and Methods* (New Delhi: Department of Statistics, Ministry of Planning, Government of India), 1989.

Chakarverty, S., "Drain Theory of Dadabhai Naoroji," a paper presented to the Indian Economic Association Conference, December, 1968.

Chandra, Bipan, *The Rise and Growth of Economic Nationalism in India, Economic Policies of Indian National Leadership 1880-1905* (New Delhi: People's Publishing House), 1966.

Charlesworth, Neil, *British Rule and the Indian Economy, 1800-1914* (London: Macmillan), 1982.

Chatterjee, D.K., *C.R. Das and Indian National* (Calcutta: Bhattachariya), 1965.

Chatterjee, R.N., *On Labour Capital* (Calcutta: Chatterjee & Co.), n.d.

Chaudhuri, K.N., "India's International Economy in the Nineteenth Century: An Historical Survey", *Modern Asian Studies*, Vol. 2, No.1 (January), 1968.

Chintamani, C.Y., *Speeches and Writings of Sir Pherozeshah Mehta* (Allahabad: The Indian Press), 1905.

Chintamani, C.Y., *Indian Politics Since the Mutiny* (New Delhi: Rupa), 2002.

Chiplunkar, Vishnushastri, *Nibandh Mula* (Poona: S.V. Bapat), 1926.

Chirol, Valentine, *Indian Unrest* (London: Macmillan), 1910.

Coase, R.H., *Essays on Economics and Economists* (Chicago: The University of Chicago Press), 1994.

Clark, Colin, *Conditions of Economic Progress* (London: MacMillan and Co. Ltd.), 1949.

Dantwala, M.L., *Poverty in India, Then and Now, 1870-1970* (Delhi: MacMillan), 1973.

Das, C.R. and Bhagwan Das, *Outline Scheme of Swaraj* (Bombay: Swastik), 1923.

Das, M.N., *Indian National Congress Versus the British*, Vol. 1, (1885-1918), Delhi, 1978.

Dasgupta, Ajit K., *A History of Indian Economic Thought* (London: Routledge), 1993.

Dasgupta, Hemendranath, *Deshbandhu Chittaranjan Das* (New Delhi: Publications Division, Ministry of Information and Broadcasting, Government of India), 1960.

Datta, Bhabatosh, *Indian Economic Thought – Twentieth Century Perspectives* (New Delhi: Tata McGraw Hill Publishing Company Ltd.), 1962.

Datta, Bhabatosh, *The Evolution of Economic Thinking in India* (Dr. P.N. Banerjea Memorial Lectures, 1961) (Calcutta: Federation Hall Society), 1962.

Desai, S.S.M., *Economic History of India* (New Delhi: Himalaya Publishing House), 1990.

Deogirikar, T.R., *Gopal Krishna Gokhale* (New Delhi: Publications Division, Ministry of Information and Broadcasting, Government of India), 1950.

Dimand, Robert W., "I have no Great Faith in Political Arithmetick: Adam Smith and Quantitative Political Economy" in *Measurement, Quantification and Economic Analysis: Numeracy in Economics* edited by Ingrid H. Rima (London: Routledge), 1995.

Dutt, R., Palme, *India Today* (Delhi: People's Publishing House), 1955,

Dutt, Romesh, *The Economic History of India Under the British Rule*, Vols. 1, 2 & 3 (New Delhi: Publications Division, Ministry of Information and Broadcasting, Government of India), 1963.

Dwyer, M.O., *India as I Knew It* (London: Seluryin Blornt), 1935.

Gandhi, M.K., *An Autobiography or The Story of My Experiments With Truth* (Ahmedabad: Navajivan Publishing House), 1942.

Gandhi, M.K., *Constructive Programme: Its Meaning and Scope* (Ahmedabad: Navajivan Publishing House), 1952.

Gandhi, M.K., *Gokhale – My Political Guru* (Ahmedabad: Navajivan Publishing House), 1952.

Ganguli, B.N., *Dadabhai Naoroji and the Drain Theory* (New York: Asia Publishing House), 1965.

Ganguli, B.N., *Indian Economic Thought: Nineteenth Century Perspectives* (New Delhi: Tata McGraw-Hill Publishing Co. Ltd.), 1978.

Georgescu-Roegen, Nicholas, *Analytical Economics: Issues and Problems* (Cambridge, Massachusetts: Harvard University Press), 1966.

Ghose, Aurobindo, *Bankim-Tilak-Dayananda* (Calcutta: Arya Publishing House), 1940.

Ghose, Aurobindo, *The Foundations of Indian Culture* (New York: The Sri Aurobindo Library),1953.

Ghose, Aurobindo, *The Ideal of the Karmayogin* (Pondicherry: Sri Aurobindo Ashram),1950.

Gopalakrishnan, P.K., *Development of Economic Ideas in India, 1880-1914* (Gravenhange: Institute of Social Studies), 1954.

Gupta, Ajit Das, *A History of Indian Economic Thought* (Madras: T.R. Publications Private Limited), 1990.

Ingrid H. Rima (ed.), *Measurement, Quantification and Economic Analysis: Numeracy in Economics* (London: Routledge), 1995.

Iyer, C.S. Ranga, *India in the Crucible* (London: Seluryin Blornt), 1928.

Jayakar, M.R., *The Story of My Life*, Vol. I (Bombay: Asia Publishing House), 1958.

Jenk, L.H., "British Experience with Foreign Investments," *Journal of Economic History*, 1944.

Jha, Shiva Chandra, *A History of Indian Economic Thought* (Calcutta: Firma K. L. Mukhopadhyay), 1981.

Jog, N.G., *Lokmanya Bal Gangadhar Tilak* (New Delhi: Publications Division, Ministry of Information and Broadcasting, Government of India), 1962.

Karmakar, A.D., *Economic Thought of Modern India* (Dharwar: J.S.S., Institute of Economic Research), 1974.

Karunakaran, K.P., *Indian Politics From Dadabhai Naoroji to Gandhi: A Study of the Political Ideas of Modern India* (New Delhi: Gitanjali Publishing House), 1988.

Kelkar, N.C. *Landmarks in Lokamanya's Life* (Madras: Ganesan & Co.), 1924.

Khan, Sir Syed Ahmad, *The Complete Collection of Lectures and Speeches* (ed.) by M.I. Gujarati (Lahore: Nawal Kishore), n.d.

Knight, Robert, *India: A Review of England's Financial Relations Therewith* (London: W.J. Johnson), 1968.

Kulkarni, A.V., *Lokmanya Tilak* (Bombay: Inderprakash Steam Press), 1909.

Kurdas, Cigdern, "The Whig Historian on Adam Smith: Paul Samuelson's Canonical Model", *History of Economics Society Bulletin*, Vol. X, No. 1 (Spring), 1988.

Lakatos, Imre, "Falsification and the Methodology of Scientific Research Programmes" in *Criticism and the Growth of Knowledge* edited by Imre Lakatos and Alan Musgrave (Cambridge: Cambridge University Press), 1970.

Lipton, Michael and Ravallion, Martin, "Poverty and Policy", Policy Research Working Papers, No. WPS 1130 (Washington: The World Bank), 1993.

Loganathan, *A History of Economic Thought* (New Delhi: S. Chand and Company Ltd.), 1987.

Madan, G.R., *Economic Thinking in India* (Madras: S. Chand & Co.), 1982

Mahajan, O.P., *The Drain Theory: Fact and Fiction* (IEA), 1968.

Majumdar, Jatindra Kumar (ed.), *Indian Speeches and Documents on British Rule, 1821-1918* (London), 1937.

Masani, R.P., *Builders of Modern India—Dadabhai Naoroji* (New Delhi: Publications Division, Ministry of Information and Broadcasting, Government of India), 1960.

Masani, R.P., *Dadabhai Naoroji: The Grand Old Man of India* (London: George Allen and Unwin Ltd.), 1939.

Masani, R.P., *Dadabhai Naoroji* (New Delhi: Publications Division, Ministry of Information and Broadcasting, Government of India), 1960.

Max Karl and Fredrick Engels, *On Colonialism* (Moscow: Progress Publishers), 1965.

Mill, John Stuart, *Principles of Political Economy*, edited by W.J. Ashley (London: Longmans, Green and Co.), 1909.

Minto, *Many Countries of India, Minto and Morley 1905-1910* (London: Macmillan), 1934.

Mody, Homi, *Sir Pherozeshah Mehta* (Bombay: Asia Publishing House), 1963.

Mody, Homi, *Pherozeshah Mehta* (New Delhi: Publications Division, Ministry of Information and Broadcasting, Government of India), 1963.

Morrison Sir, Theodore, *Economic Transition in India* (London: London Press), 1916.

Mukherjee, M., *National Income of India Trends and Structure* (Calcutta: Statistical Publishing Society), 1969.

Mukerjee, Tapan, "Theory of Economic Drain: Impact of British Rule on the Indian Economy: 1840-1900" in *Economic Imperialism: A Book of Readings*, edited by K.E. Boulding and Tapan Mukherjee (Ann Arbor: The University of Michigan Press), 1972.

Nabers, Lawrence, 'The Positive and Genetic Approaches' in *The Structure of Economic Science Essays on Methodology*, edited by Sherman Roy Krupp (Englewood Cliffs, N.J.: Prentice-Hall, Inc.), 1966.

Nanda, B.R., *Gokhale* (Delhi: Oxford University Press), 1977.

Nanda, B.R., *Gokhale, Gandhi and the Nehru's Studies in Indian Nationalism* (London: George Allen and Unwin Ltd.), 1990.

Nanda, B.R., *Three`Statesmen Gokhale, Gandhi and Nehru* (Delhi: Oxford University Press), 2004.

Naoroji, Dadabhai, *A Sketch of his Life and Career* (Madras: G.A. Natesan & Co.), 1920.

Naoroji, Dadabhai, Speeches and Writings of Dadabhai Naoroji (Madras: G.A. Natesan & Co.), n.d.

Naoroji, Dadabhai, *The Financial Administration of India* (London: W.J. Johnson), 1871.

Naoroji, Dadabhai, *Essays, Speeches, Addresses and Writings* (Bombay: Caxton Printing Works), 1899.

Naoroji, Dadabhai, *Poverty and Un-British Rule in India* (New Delhi: Publications Division, Government of India), 1962.

Naoroji, Dadabhai, *India's Wrongs and Remedy* (Madras: The Commonwealth Office), 1917.

Nehru, Jawaharlal, *Autobiography* (London: The Bodley Head), 1947.

Okakura, *Ideals of the East* (Calcutta: Editions Indian), 1973.

Pal, Bepin Chandra, *His Life and Utterances* (Madras: Ganesan & Co.), 1925.

Pandey, Shridhar, *Economic History of India* (Hindi), (Patna: Motilal Banarsidas), 1991.

Parekh C.L., *Essays, Speeches, Address and Writings (on Indian Politics) of the Hon'ble Dadabhai Naoroji* (Bombay: Asia Publishers), 1887.

Parliamentary Debates (House of Commons) Fourth Series Vol. XI, 13th April 1893.

Parvate, T.V., *Bal Gangadhar Tilak* (Ahmedabad: Navajivan Publishing House), 1958.

Parvate, T.V., *Gopal Krishna Gokhale* (Ahmedabad: Navajivan Publishing House), 1958.

Patwardhan, R.P. (ed.), *Dadabhai Naoroji Correspondence, Child and Youth Section*, Vol. II, Part I (Bombay: Allied Publishers), 1977.

Paul, R.R., *History of Economic Thought* (New Delhi: Kalyani Publishers), 1979.

Pradhan, G.P. and A.K. Bhagwat, *Lokmanya Tilak: A Biography* (Poona: J.S. Tilak), 1963.

Prasad, R., *At the Feet of Mahatma Gandhi* (Bombay: Asia Publishing House), 1961.

Price Powell, *A History of India* (London: Thomas Nelson and Sons Limited), 1955.

Ranade, Mahadev Govind, *Ranade's Economic Writings,* edited by Bipan Chandra (New Delhi: Gian Publishing House), 1990.

Rao, V.K.R.V., *An Essay on India's National Income, 1925-1929* (London: George Allen and Unwin), 1939.

Rashid, Salim, "Does a Famous Economist Deserve Special Standards? A Critical Note on Adam Smith Scholarship," *History of Economics Society Bulletin*, Vol. XI, No. 2 (Fall), 1989.

Ray, M.N., *India in Transition* (Bombay: Nachiketa), 1971.

Ray, P.C., *Life and Times of C.R. Das* (Calcutta: Orient Books), 1958.

Robinson, Joan, *An Essay on Marxian Economics* (London: Macmillan), 1966.

Rogin, Leo, *The Meaning and Validity of Economic Theory* (New York: Harper and Bros.), 1956.

Ronaldshay, *Earl of the Heart of Aryavrata: A Study of the Psychology of Indian Unrest* (London: Constable), 1925.

Saggi, P.D. (ed.), *Life and Work of Lal, Bal and Pal* (New Delhi: Overseas Publishing House), 1962.

Samuelson, Paul, "The Transfer Problem and Transport Costs: The Terms of Trade when Impediments are Absent," *Economic Journal*, Vol. LXII, No. 246 (June), 1952.

Samuelson, Paul, "Out of the Closet: A Program for the Whig History of Economic Science", *History of Economics Society Bulletin*, IKI (Fall), 1987.

Sastri, V.S. Srinivasa, *Life and Times of Sir Pherozeshah Mehta* (Bangalore: Bangalore Printing Co.), 1937.

Sastri, V.S. Srinivasa, *My Master Gokhale* (Madras: Model Publications), 1946.

Sastri, V.S.S., *Life of Gopal Krishna Gokhale* (Bangalore: Bangalore Printing Co.), 1937.

Schumpeter, J.A., *History of Economic Analysis* (New York: Oxford University Press), 1954.

Scweinitz Jr. Karl de, *The Rise and Fall of British India: Imperialism as Inequality* (London: Methuen & Co.), 1983.

Selected Essays of Sister Nivedita (Madras: Ganesan & Co.), 1911.

Sen, R.K. and Mandal, S.K., *Ranade's Analysis of India's Population Problem and The Views of Naoroji and Doskar*, I.E.A., 75th Conference Volume, 1992.

Sen, Rathindra Nath, *Life and Times of Deshbandhu Chittranjan Das* (New Delhi: Northern Book Centre), 1989.

Sen, Sunanda, *Colonies and the Empire India, 1890-1914* (Hyderabad: Orient Longman), 1922.

Shanmugasundaram, V., *Indian Economic Thought and Policy* (New Delhi: S. Chand and Company Ltd.), 1981.

Sharma, Jai Narain, *Power, Politics and Corruption: A Gandhian Solution* (New Delhi: Deep and Deep), 2005.

Sharma, Jai Narain, "Gandhi and the Congress Presidents" in Malhotra, S.C. (ed.) *Gandhi and the Indian National*

Congress (Chandigarh: Publications Bureau, Panjab University), 1988

Shay, Theodore, *The Legacy of Lokmanya* (London: Oxford University Press), 1956.

Singh, V.B., *From Naoroji to Nehru* (New Delhi: MacMillan), 1975.

Sitaramayya, Pattabhi, *History of Indian National Congress 1885-1935*, Vol. I (New Delhi: S. Chand & Co.), 1969.

Spear, T.G.P., *India* (London: Seluryin Blornt), 1935.

Speeches and Writings of Gopal Krishna Gokhale (New York: Asia Publishing House), 1966.

Stark, Werner, *The History of Economics in its Relation to Social Development* (London: Kegan Paul, Trench, Trubner & Co.), 1944.

Studenski, Paul, *The Income of Nations* (New York: New York University Press), 1958.

Tilak, B.G., *Gita Rahasya* (Poona: Tilak Brothers), 1925.

Tilak, B.G., *His Writings and Speeches* (Madras: Ganeshan & Co.), 1922.

Tilak, B.G., *Samagra Lokmanya Tilak*, Vol. IV (Pune: Kesari Prakashan), 1974.

Varma, V.P., *Modern Indian Political Thought* (Agra: Lakshmi Narain Agarwal), 1961.

Vaswani, T.L., *India in Chains* (Madras: Ganesan & Co.), 1920.

Viner, Jacob, *Studies in the Theory of International Trade* (London: George Allen and Unwin), 1960.

Wolpert Stanley, *Tilak and Gokhale* (Berkeley: University of California Press), 1962.

World Bank, *World Development Report, 1990* (Oxford: Oxford University Press), 1990.

Zachaias, H.C.E., *Renascent India* (London: Allen), 1933.

Zaidi, A.M. et al., *The Encycolpaedia of Indian National Congress* (New Delhi: S. Chand & Co.), 1980

Zaidi Moin A., *Dadabhai Naoroji, Speeches and Writings* (New Delhi: Indian Institute of Applied Political Research), Vol. 1, 1985.

Index